ANTI-ABORTIONIST AT LARGE

How to Argue Intelligently About Abortion and Live to Tell About It

By

Raymond Dennehy

TRAFFORD

National Library of Canada Cataloguing in Publication

Dennehy, Raymond Leo, 1934-
    Anti-abortionist at large : how to argue intelligently about abortion and live to tell about it / Raymond Dennehy.

Includes bibliographical references and index.
ISBN 1-55369-380-9

    1. Dennehy, Raymond Leo, 1934- 2. Pro-life movement.
3. Abortion—Moral and ethical aspects. I. Title.

HQ767.15.D45 2002   363.46   C2002-901508-1

TRAFFORD

This book was published *on-demand* in cooperation with Trafford Publishing.
On-demand publishing is a unique process and service of making a book available for retail sale to the public taking advantage of on-demand manufacturing and Internet marketing.
On-demand publishing includes promotions, retail sales, manufacturing, order fulfilment, accounting and collecting royalties on behalf of the author.

Suite 6E, 2333 Government St., Victoria, B.C. V8T 4P4, CANADA
Phone   250-383-6864   Toll-free   1-888-232-4444 (Canada & US)
Fax   250-383-6804   E-mail   sales@trafford.com
Web site   www.trafford.com   TRAFFORD PUBLISHING IS A DIVISION OF TRAFFORD HOLDINGS LTD.
Trafford Catalogue #02-0193   www.trafford.com/robots/02-0193.html

10   9   8   7   6   5   4

FOR MAGGIE MOUSE

"Many other times have I said it, and now I say it again; a knight errant without a lady is like a tree without leaves, a building without foundations, and a shadow without a body to account for it."

— *The Adventures of Don Quixote,* Pt. II, Ch. XXXII

ACKNOWLEDGEMENTS

I begin with an expression of special gratitude to Rev. James Schall of Georgetown University. Without him, this book probably never would have been written. Besides reading the manuscript and proposing valuable suggestions, it was he who urged me, in the first place, to write a book on my experiences as an anti-abortion debater. My debt to John Hamlon is great, not only for his line-by-line scrutiny of the manuscript and stylistic suggestions, but also for his encouragement before and during the project. I am greatly indebted to Roxanne Lum for her generosity and artistry in designing the book's cover, offering guidance in the selection of page-layout, and proposing not only that there be a sub-title but also for proposing the sub-title. I am also greatly indebted to Erasmo Leiva-Merikakis for his generosity and linguistic mastery in providing new English translations of the passages from *Don Quixote* that adorn the opening of each chapter. I am grateful to Sharon Tyree, Kim Summerhays, and Ed Kaitz for reading the manuscript and offering valuable suggestions; to Michael Torre for calling attention to a muddled passage in the manuscript's preface and to Steven Consiglio for practical advice. I must also acknowledge my gratitude to the following: Rev. Francis Filice, founder and first head of United For Life in San Francisco. Kevin and Sheila Starr for their friendship and generosity over the years, especially during the first important writing project of my life, my doctoral dissertation, Dan and Carmen Williams, the Rev. Robert Maloney, S.J., the Rev. C. M. Buckley, S.J., the Rev. Charles Dullea, S.J., and the Rev. Joseph Fessio, S.J., John and Mary Galten, Kathy Hamlon, Tony and Judy Simon, Mireya Letayf, Tom and Bonnie Cavanaugh, Desmond and Evelyn Fitzgerald, and my children, Mark, Bridget, Andrea, and Rosalind. But I am most grateful to Maryann, my wife and best friend, for her loving support throughout, her proof reading of the final draft, and her frank comments.

Raymond Dennehy
San Francisco

CREDITS

CONTENTS

PREFACE

"'I'm telling you, my lord,' said Sancho, 'that those things over there are not giants but windmills, and what appears to be their arms are the sails which the wind moves and which make the millstone turn.'

'It's evident,' replied Don Quixote, 'that you don't have much experience in this matter of adventures. They are *giants*; and, if you're afraid, get out of the way and start praying while I encounter them in fierce and unequal battle.'"

—*Miguel Cervantes, The Adventures of Don Quixote, Pt.I, Ch. VIII*

Sometimes I feel as if we "pro-lifers" are Don Quixotes jousting with windmills. But there are differences. For one thing, we know that the giants are the illusion and the windmills the reality. So why joust? We do it because we can't destroy the giants without combating the windmills. But why bother with the giants if they are only an illusion? The answer to that question is what this book is all about – a tale of trying to destroy an illusion.

We're not, by a long shot, the only ones who know it's an illusion. Many people, most notably the purveyors of the illusion, have a vested interest in keeping it going. And the vast majority of people are so used to seeing the giants that they now accept them as a normal part of their social horizon. So if we can destroy the giants, we can expose their purveyors for what they are – death mongers who need deceit to continue their mongering. Hopefully, it will also prompt all the others to remind themselves that it won't do – not for the future of our democratic society, not for civilization – for us to keep going on treating the illusion as if it were the reality.

All of which brings up another difference between Don Quixote and us pro-lifers. The illusion we're attacking isn't giants; it's "fetuses". And the

9

reality here isn't windmills, but the idea of unborn babies.

Like the man from La Mancha, we seem, if not mad, then at least comical. But, once again, the similarity doesn't hide the difference. For here things are reversed. Don Quixote lived a life of fantasy, mistaking illusion for reality. All his reading about the knights errant of old and their chivalrous deeds finally took control of his mind and, indeed, his entire being, so that when he looked at the jejune and the commonplace, he saw villainy and the call to knightly valor: Shepherds and their sheep were legions of enemy soldiers; a barber's metallic water basin was Mambrino's helmet, a common, rough-hewn peasant girl, one Aldonza Lorenzo from the village of El Toboso, was the elegant and beautiful aristocratic lady, Dulcinea del Toboso, to whom he would forever remain faithful and for whose honor he was ready to perform the most heroic deeds; and a sagging, bag-of-bones of a nag, long since put out to pasture, was the noble steed, Rocinante.

Crazy Don Quixote! Poster boy for the heroic life he ain't. One interpretation of the Don's adventures is that Cervantes intended them as a satire of Charles V's efforts to preserve the nobility of Spain's past by resisting his country's entrance into the modern age. Yet, the huge attraction readers have had for him down through the centuries can hardly be reduced to the comedy produced by his insane mimicry of knight errantry. We are drawn to the figure of Don Quixote for another reason as well. His readings of the romanticized accounts of chivalry, despite all their fictional and fantastic trappings, called his attention to what civilization had lost – its idealism, adherence to virtue, and the readiness to risk death in their defense. It was the Don's estimate that the wicked attack virtue more than the good defend it.

Not even the dogged efforts of Sancho Panza, his bewildered yet devoted traveling companion, could persuade him that he'd mistaken the fanciful for the real. Yet, why would Sancho, with all the hardheaded practical sense of his peasant class, choose to leave his wife and daughter to serve so daft a leader? Thereby hangs a tale. He hoped for material gain. Despite his practicality, he remained simple-minded enough to believe that Don Quixote would reward his loyal service by making him governor of an isle. But alongside this simple-minded hope for material riches and power, Sancho shared his master's ideals. For when he finally got his chance to govern an isle – hoodwinked though he was by a decadently bored royal couple – he exercised his power with a surprising Solomon-like wisdom and justice, showing little concern for worldly riches or glory. Don Quixote was a lunatic, but his was a lunacy of the high-minded sort, a strain to which only men and women who pride themselves on being in tune with the "real world" can claim immunity.

There is still another difference that separates Don Quixote from pro-lifers: If the refusal to accept reality is the mark of madness, then the critics of abortion are sane and it's the pro-abortionists who seem mad. Anti-abortionists see the difference between reality and illusion; it's the pro-abortionists who speak and act as though the illusion were the reality.

I do not think it presumptuous, in this case, to speak for others in the pro-life movement and say that, despite all these differences, we would revel in feelings of identity with the Knight from La Mancha. I believe the similarities counterbalance the differences. Like Don Quixote, we seem impervious to "common sense" and the "new morality," deaf to the voices of people who tell us that we are out of touch with reality. I remember once, while debating abortion at the University of California at Berkeley, a young woman in the audience asked me, "How does it feel to defend a position that the majority of Americans disagree with?" I replied that, in the first place, I wasn't convinced that the majority favored abortion on request, but that even if that were the case, I'd continue to speak against abortion, to argue that the unborn are human beings, not clumps of cells, and to insist that it is a perverse liberation that depends on killing defenseless, unborn children.

I see another similarity between Don Quixote and us pro-lifers. He was committed to defending the chivalric code even if it meant his life. Now I must confess that, in all my years as an anti-abortionist, I never had the sense that my life was in danger. That is just as well, because we professors are a timid lot. We like to wage war, but only in our heads. If my life were ever threatened, I would hope that I would nevertheless continue to speak against abortion. (Words can't express how grateful I am that the issue has never arisen.) Still, my timorous self notwithstanding, I've committed myself to the proposition that the right to life, especially the right of the innocent and helpless to life, is the foundation of democratic society and, more broadly, Western civilization. Right from the start of the abortion controversy, in the late 1950s, we saw what was at stake: the way the American people address the issue of legalized abortion will determine whether or not American democracy will perish from the earth. Don Quixote saw the chivalric code as foundational to the defense of civilization's ideals. We see the right to life in the same way. He lamented the loss of heroic ideals. I, and my cohorts, lament the erosion of spiritual and ethical ideals — like the existence of God and his absolute sovereignty over creation, the dignity of each human person and the objective nature of ethical principles.

A couple more similarities. I'd love to ride into battle (you know, debate abortion) atop a magnificent steed, that is, have the support of the legislators, judges, scientists, professors and the media. The truth is that I, and almost all who struggle against legalized abortion, found out early on that broken down nags would be our common form of conveyance. We could never count on much financing, no matter what tales you might have heard from pro-abortionists about massive transfusions of money from the Catholic Church. Financial support was not the only thing we lacked. The media were always shamelessly biased in favor of abortion and our elected officials have, from the start, done so much flip-flopping to avoid giving a clear statement of where they stand on abortion they have no doubt kept the chiropractors working overtime, kneading and pounding the kinks and twists out of their spines. The saddest thing of all is the way the clergy – I have in mind Catholic priests and bishops – have been so willing to leave those of us in the pro-life movement twisting in the wind. The silence from the Sunday pulpit has been thunder in our ears.

All in all, we were always a rag-tag lot. When the public debate began, the pro-abortionists probably saw us as more of an annoyance than a threat. But now we have more legal, political, medical and academic support. The increase in the number of pro-life legislators has given us much needed muscle. Still, anybody who's been around the anti-abortion movement knows that its membership comes mostly from the ranks of the working class: many housewives and retired men and women, usually with no more than a high school education.

We may look abject and comical like "the Knight of the Sad Countenance," but there's something glorious and invigorating in struggling "to right the unrightable wrong, to beat the unbeatable foe" – especially when, as the last twenty-five years have shown, the wrong isn't so unrightable and the foe not so unbeatable.

Don Quixote set out on his mission to restore the virtues of the chivalrous life with a long tree branch for a lance, a suit of rusty old armor for which he had to fashion a make-shift helmet, and an old nag to carry him about. He wasn't in such great shape himself. Still, the knight teaches a practical lesson: if you must rise to a challenge, you've got to make do with what's at hand.

"Hi, Ho Rocinante! Away!"

INTRODUCTION

"I am Don Quixote de la Mancha, and my other name is the Knight of the Sad Countenance. Although praise of self is demeaning, I am forced at times to engage in it, which is understandable when no one else does it. And so, my dear sir, now that you know who I am and what my profession is, nothing about me should astound you: neither this horse nor this spear, neither this shield nor this squire, neither the bulk of all these arms nor the sallowness of my face nor the excessive thinness of my form."

The Adventures of Don Quixote, Pt. II, Ch. XVI

This book is an autobiographical account of almost four decades of publicly speaking against, and debating on, induced abortion. Because much of this narrative unfolds in the context of my association with pro-life groups, the book is unavoidably also an anecdotal history of the pro-life movement in America, a movement that parallels in importance the anti-slavery movement of the 19th century. The book is equally a manual for debating against abortion. This, too, was the inevitable consequence of writing an autobiography. For my purpose in writing it, in the first place, was to share my experiences of speaking out on what has to be the most controversial topic of the past few decades. Squaring off against an opponent, who may be an expert in the field of science or law or medicine and doing it in front of a large audience many of whom, perhaps most, not only disagree with you but dislike you before you've even had a chance to open your mouth, teaches you things about debating abortion that you can't learn in any other way.

I've arranged the chapters in the following way. Chapters 1-4 tell how I got into the public debate on abortion and, in so doing, give the anecdotal history of the pro-life movement; Chapters 5, 6 and 7 are the "how-to" part; Chapter 8 is quite different from the preceding chapters, as it offers my speculation on the mythic significance of the pro-abortion movement in our culture. I've included in the appendices a sampling of the letters sent me by people present at my debates to give some idea of typical responses to my anti-abortion argument.

Before I conceived of this project, it never occurred to me that it would be something I would ever undertake. As a philosophy professor, I assumed that the kinds of things I would always write would be theoretical and speculative, replete with analyses of words and concepts, with thorough and even tortured critiques of the arguments and theories found in philosophy books and scholarly journals. But once committed to the writing of this book, I knew I was entering a realm of discourse that was foreign to me: personal narrative, a story about my life as an anti-abortion debater in the public forum, about what it's like for a "professor" to take the more unpopular side of a hot-button topic on television, radio, and before various groups in the community at large. My entry into the public arena disabused me of the assumptions nourished in the hothouse environments of graduate school and the university classroom. I came to realize that the lofty, rational discussions that Plato celebrates in his *Dialogues* are not what you could expect to encounter when addressing a popular, often unprofessional audience, especially on a hot-button topic like abortion. Arguments there hardly ever run with Socratic smoothness and you can't count on your opponents' or even your supporters' objectivity.

The persona needed for the public forum requires some sacrifice of rigor in argument and thoroughness in analysis. I don't mean to sound snobbish. But the fact is the vast majority of people, no matter how intelligent, lead practical lives and are simply not comfortable breathing the thin air of abstract theories and logic. The luxury of reflecting on and discussing the great thoughts of civilization that academics enjoy is not available to them.

Although many of my abortion gigs take place on university campuses, even then the atmosphere and requirements are different from those of the classroom or learned societies and more like addressing an audience outside the university. For example, one of my frequent campus visits is in a course that typically has 700 students in its audience and is held in a large auditorium. The students who comprise those audiences are, for the most part, smart and expect reasoned, informed arguments, as well as emotional restraint; yet I find that they're often in the grip of ideologies but don't know it or if they do know it somehow don't feel obliged to justify them. To some extent, their intransigence can be attributed to the fact that most of them have not had any courses in philosophy, specifically ethics, or logic.

Still, I don't think that that explanation gets to the heart of the intransigence. For that you have to acknowledge the social power of ideology over reason. Early on I found to my astonishment that, appeals to the embryological sciences not withstanding, the students' responses were, on the whole, predictable: "But what about women's rights?" "A sixteen year-old's life would be ruined if she had to have the baby and drop out of school." "The fetus is part of the woman's body so she can do whatever she wants with it." "An unwanted child's life will be miserable; he or she would be better off dead." Alongside such mantras, reasonable questions like, "Is induced abortion the deliberate killing of an innocent human being?" and "If so, what happens to a society that legalizes the deliberate killing of the unborn?" fade into the misty world of the irrelevant.

All this is not to suggest that I harbor illusions about the freedom of my pro-abortion academic colleagues from ideology. I do not. In Chapter 8 I air my persisting suspicion that they are simply more adept at covering their ideological commitments under clever and often brilliant arguments to the effect that the embryo lacks moral significance because it is not yet sentient or that the fetus, and even the infant, have no claim to a right to life because they have yet to display the activities that count for personhood. At all events, this book is about the people I've debated and the audiences I've addressed, hardly any of whom have been academics.

In addition to being an autobiography, an anecdotal history, and a debate manual, this book has a forth characteristic, one with special meaning for me. It's my story, but it is more than my story; it is my personal testament. Looking back on an otherwise undistinguished career as a teacher and scholar in philosophy, I find that all my years of publicly criticizing induced abortion surround an otherwise ambiguous existence with an aura of Socratic redemption. I needn't be reminded, "the gadfly of the San Francisco Bay Area" doesn't have the same ring as "the gadfly of Athens"; but it would surely make a more honorific epitaph than, "He was respected by his fellow members of the American Philosophical Association." At all events, I allow myself the indulgence of Socratic fantasies. Like a generous layer of cream cheese on a day old bagel, they make an academic's routine palatable.

CHAPTER ONE

NO ONE'S EVER ACCUSED ME
OF BEING BRILLIANT

"Well protected by his shield and with the spear in its rest, he then charged ahead with Rocinante at full gallop and attacked the first windmill he came to. He dealt it a spear thrust in the sail, which the wind began turning with such fury that it shattered the spear to pieces, pulling in its wake both horse and horseman, and the latter rolled across the field sorely wounded."

The Adventures of Don Quixote, Pt. I, Ch. VIII

In this chapter, I offer examples of what I meant when I wrote in the introduction that my entry into the public debate on abortion disabused me of the assumptions I acquired in graduate school about the prevalence of open-minded, reasonable discussion.

CONFRONTING TROUBLED STUDENTS

In 1969, I accepted an invitation to speak at Mayfield High School in Palo Alto, a town about thirty miles south of San Francisco. Whatever the reason, the name, "Mayfield," conjured images in me of an upscale middle class school, more preppy than public. I drove there filled with anticipations of well-bred, civil students, but I arrived to discover that the school had been converted into a continuation school for troubled teenagers. My audience was anything but civil; certainly not well behaved. As soon as I entered the classroom, I knew they didn't like me. I was another authority figure. There was not just one teacher in this class of twenty or thirty students as you might expect, but three.

While I was speaking, one student began threatening audibly that he was going to punch that "m___f___r"(me!). I pretended not to notice, but my heart was pounding. I kept thinking, "What am I going to do if he charges me?" One of the teachers finally managed to quiet him. Prozac wasn't on the market then. During the discussion period that followed, one rather hulking student blurted, in a voice charged with emotion and hurt, "I wish my mother had aborted me!" Apparently events in his life at home persuaded him he was unloved: "When my younger brother asked for a bike, they got him a brand new one; but when I asked for one, they got me a second hand bike."

Another student, in response to my statement that you can't use words like "person" in an ethical dispute without producing a reasonably clear definition, took a dictionary down from one of the shelves and looked up "person." Reading aloud its definition, which seemed to him to differ from mine, a triumphal grin crossed his face. That was not the last time in the session that he consulted the dictionary, clearly hoping to contradict me. Obviously, he was not interested in checking definitions to be precise or for his own elucidation. He was determined to trip me up for the sake of tripping me up.

After it was all over, one young man approached the podium to talk with me; he had the innocent, clean-cut look of a choir boy. He told me: "When my mother heard that you were coming here to speak against abortion, she told me I'd better be against abortion." Then he added, "That f___ing whore." This was not just a hard audience; it was group therapy run amok. It wasn't my anti-abortion stance that led these students to oppose me. To them, I was just another authority figure, an adult who had to be kept at bay.

MY FIRST RADIO GIG

"What am I doing here? Why did I volunteer to speak against abortion on the radio?" Like a merry-go-round that was not so merry, these questions kept circling in my head. As the minutes ticked away before going on the air, the fear and feelings of inadequacy that I'd been wrestling with all morning in anticipation of the event were getting the better of me. Maybe you remember a television commercial that featured a young man trying to create the impression of fiscal sobriety for the bank's customer service representative while opening his first account. His constant shifting in his seat, while the banker explained the various checking plans to him, only heightened his already conspicuous insecurity. Suddenly, his clip-on necktie came undone and the pre-tied knot slipped midway down his shirt, exposing his inexperience with neckties. As I waited in the reception area of the radio station, I felt like a "clip-on" professor. My mounting insecurity finally persuaded me that, at any moment while I was on the air, my semblance of knowledge about the ethics of abortion would pop open, exposing me before a large listening audience as an incompetent. I berated myself for soliciting this gig in the first place. What, after all, could I say against abortion that would be incisive and important?

It was 1970. Although the U.S. Supreme Court's *Roe v. Wade* decision was still three years away, the public debate over legalized abortion had reached the boiling point in the late 1960s. It seems a radio listener had approached the producers of a popular radio talk show in the San Francisco Bay Area, "The Joe Dolan Show" (KGO), about having an anti-abortion speaker as one of its guests. The producer of the show contacted the leader of one of the local pro-life groups in my area who, in turn, persuaded me to let the producers know that I was available to fill that role. I did, and the station invited me to appear on the show. That would be my first experience with an audience — and a very large one to boot – that was more hostile than not to what I would say.

About fifteen minutes before show time, a staff worker ushered me into the "Green Room." That's where the show's guests waited to be called into the broadcast booth. "Make yourself comfortable," she invited, pointing to the faded red sofa. "There's coffee and tea, but we're all out of pastry; sorry. Joe Dolan's on vacation. Your host today will be Robin King;

he'll be in shortly to chat with you. You'll like him; he's a really nice guy."
She turned and walked out of the room, leaving me alone again with my
alter ego, Incompetence. I exchanged stares with the glaring red light on
the coffee maker. The last thing I needed now was caffeine.

A few minutes later, Robin King entered the room. "Professor Dennehy,
I'm Robin King; thanks for coming on the show." The jovial greeting
came with the offer of a handshake " "My pleasure," I replied as we shook
hands. A middle-aged man of medium height and a touch overweight,
with gray, wavy hair, mustache and goatee, he reminded me of those distinguished 19th century generals and statesmen that you see on Italian
currency and Austrian postage stamps. What really grabbed my attention
was his voice – soothingly deep and mellow. The staff member was right.
He seemed like a really nice guy.

A few seconds of chitchat and I was already feeling more at ease, but
that didn't last long. It ended when he asked: "How do you want to be
called, 'Professor,' 'Doctor'?" I hadn't finished my doctoral dissertation yet
so I didn't have my Ph.D.; I wasn't a doctor; and, at the University of
Santa Clara, where I was teaching, that meant I wasn't even an assistant
professor; I was a lowly "instructor." Still, I didn't want to be called "Mr.
Dennehy" or "Ray" because I wanted to speak with the learned authority
of a professor. I quickly rationalized to myself that I was a professor in the
generic sense of the term; after all, I was a full time teacher of philosophy
at a university. Sheepishly, I replied, "My family prefers that I use the title,
'Professor,' when I speak in public." I just couldn't bring myself to tell the
truth and say I wanted to be called "Professor"; it seemed so pompous.
Besides, I didn't feel very much like a professor at the moment. So I
placed the responsibility for preferring the title of professor on my family.

King glanced at the clock on the wall. I followed his example. It was
10 minutes to three. "It's time," he said. We got up from the sofa and, as we
proceeded through the doorway, I got my first look at the broadcasting
booth. Once again, the not so merry merry-go-round circled in my head:
"What am I doing here? Why did I volunteer? I don't belong here." The
booth was enclosed in glass; it had an "s" shaped desk with two chairs,
one on each side. Each place at the desk had a microphone, the blossom
of a long rod that sprouted from the desk.

A technician introduced himself to me and then uttered an impersonal instruction to take the chair facing the glass. "Speak into the micro-

phone so we can check your sound level," he said clinically. Not knowing what to say, I just started counting, "I, 2,3,4." I felt foolish. The engineer was in the adjoining booth on the other side of the glass. He sat facing us, with his eyes peering down at the control panel in front of him, as he simultaneously turned two dials to adjust for my voice. He gave the technician a thumbs-up. The technician then told me not to lean back in my chair because that would take me too far from the microphone and not to sit too close to it either. With only minor attention from the technician, King pretty much took care of himself, situating himself in his chair, donning his earphones and speaking into the microphone to test the sound level: "Good afternoon out there. Welcome to the Joe Dolan show. This is Robin King, filling in for Joe Dolan; I'll be your host for the week."

By now I was borderline paranoid and the detached, impersonal styles of the technician and engineer only intensified my certainty that I didn't belong on the radio and that everybody there had already concluded that only a fool or a religious fanatic would go on a radio show in San Francisco to speak against abortion. It was 3 o'clock; the engineer gave the go signal with his arm and we were on the air.

King was fair to me during the entire two hours, which made my presentation much easier. (I've since been on programs where the host could not conceal his pro-abortion allegiance. One talk-show host repeatedly made statements loaded in favor of abortion; it turned out that he was the attorney for a women's pro-abortion group that had only a week earlier succeeded in persuading the court in Sacramento to invalidate a right to disclosure law, passed by the California State Legislature, designed to protect women who sought the services of the abortion clinic.) Still, it was a draining two hours; fielding questions from callers and responding to their criticisms for that length of time puts you through the emotional wringer, especially when you add the first-time-on-the-radio jitters. As I left the studio, heading for the door to the street, the man who gave the newscasts during our breaks handed me a small piece of folded paper as he walked by without saying a word. I continued walking while unfolding it; he had written: "I wish my mother had aborted me." I had a reply that I wouldn't dare utter because it seemed insensitive: "You're a big boy now; if you're unhappy with living, why don't you kill yourself?"

I left the station dissatisfied with my performance. First, the feeling that I'd wimped out gnawed at me all the way home. Instead of arguing

directly against abortion, I said that, as a society in the process of legalizing elective abortion, we hadn't spent time discussing whether the fetus is
a human being. (In the years that followed, I was able to forge that point
into a powerful debating weapon.) Second, I felt insecure about my argument, such as it was, for I hadn't checked the literature on the subject;
instead, I was content to let my daily knowledge of the popular media
guide me. And they avoided the question as if it were a fatal communicable disease.

Factually, my ground was solid. Even the scholarly literature was then
only beginning to address the status of the fetus; for example, on the pro-
abortion side, Michael Tooley's piece, "Abortion and Infanticide," (in which
he argues that neither the fetus nor the newborn is a person and hence is
not a valid claimant to the right to life) was published around 1968. But
Judith Jarvis Thomson's article, "A Defense of Abortion," did not appear
until 1971 and Mary Ann Warren's article, "The Moral and Legal Status of
Abortion," did not appear until 1973 while H. Tristram Englehardt's "Medicine and the Concept of Person" first saw the light of day in a lecture he
delivered at Georgetown University in 1974. Like Tooley and Warren, he
argued that neither the fetus nor the newborn is a person. Thomson's
argument, sophistical, though brilliantly so, does not depend on whether
the fetus is a human being or person. On the anti-abortion side, Germain
Grisez's *Abortion: the Myths, the Realities, and the Arguments* along with John
T. Noonan's widely anthologized essay, "An Almost Absolute Value in
History," were not available in print until 1970.

At all events, my point was well taken: as a society we ought to be
asking ourselves if induced abortion is not the direct killing of an innocent human being. I meant SERIOUSLY asking the question. There was
no shortage of people in the popular arena settling the question for themselves with tranquilizing pronouncements, such as "The fetus is part of
my body and I can do what I like with my body." Pro-abortion advocacy
groups, such as the National Abortion Rights Advocacy League (NARAL)
had already exerted a strong influence on the public's thinking about
abortion, but just because they were advocates for abortion, they side-
stepped any serious effort to answer the question, "Is the fetus a human
being?" And although the anti-abortion advocacy groups, such as the
National Right to Life, the Catholic Church and other religious denomi-
nations were able to reach large audiences, principally in churches and

religious schools, with their message that the fetus is a human being, their audience was nothing next to that commanded by the print and electronic media, whose slants were clearly pro-abortion. Although the anti-abortion book, *Handbook on Abortion*, by Dr. and Mrs. J.C. Wilke, enjoyed a wide circulation in the United States and other countries, it did not come into print until 1971 – the year following my appearance on Joe Dolan's radio program. In contrast, the influence of the popular media was then, as now, immediate, widespread, and powerful.

Still, even if I had been right in saying that we, as a society, weren't asking the right questions about the fetus, I was unhappy with my overall performance on the radio; I simply had not been cogent. My impression was that others made the same assessment. When one of my close colleagues at the university, who knew I'd be on the radio, said nothing about it, I couldn't resist asking him if he listened to the program. He replied evasively, "I heard you, Raymond, loud and clear." He volunteered nothing further. Prudence dictated that I not pursue the matter. I didn't think my mother found my performance impressive either. She offered a couple of criticisms, but said nothing positive.

Nevertheless, I consoled myself with the reminder that at least I came forward and spoke out on behalf of the unborn. There was a compensating exhilaration uttering to myself, "I did it! I'm a player in the public debate on abortion!"

MY FIRST BIG DEBATE

In 1979, I debated Mary Ann Warren on the University of San Francisco campus. Her article, "On The Moral and Legal Status of Abortion," made quite a stir among academics. It was perhaps the most frequently anthologized pro-abortion article in the scholarly literature. When the day of the debate arrived, I was scared. It wasn't as if this were my first time. I'd done a lot of public speaking on abortion before with a few debates sprinkled in. But this one was big, bigger to me than my first radio gig. It wasn't only that my opponent was Mary Ann Warren that scared me. True, she wasn't one to be taken lightly. But her husband, Michael Scriven, would be in the audience and that seemed to scare me more. When I was doing graduate studies in philosophy at the University of California at Berkeley, he was one of the heavyweights in the field. I remember him delivering a paper for the graduate philosophy club in which he argued that God could not exist. His responses to criticisms from faculty and graduate students were intimidating, all the more so because he had a gruff and physically imposing manner. I was in awe of him then and had to keep telling myself that I wasn't in awe of him now. I reminded myself that I, too, was a professor (well, at least an associate professor) and that I, too, had published works in philosophy.

But nothing put my fears to rest, not even a reminder that I was prepared. I'd studied my opponent's writings closely and even listened to a tape of a radio debate on abortion she'd had with John Noonan, then a law professor at the University of California at Berkeley. I was satisfied with the reply to her arguments that I'd forged and with my own argument against abortion. Besides, I recalled, I've got the truth on my side. Still, the picture of Scriven taking umbrage at my criticizing his wife's position and holding forth against me in his intimidating way before all those people dogged me. Anyway you sliced it, I was scared.

Evening came. I ate dinner with my family and then drove back to the university. As I walked across campus from the parking lot to McLaren Hall, the debate site, I was even more frightened than before. I realized then that it wasn't just the anticipation of Scriven sitting in the audience, after all. It was the event itself. Except for the students, this audience would not be what I'd been used to: parishioners, high school students, business and professional people and the general public you get in a radio audience. This was different. Mary Ann Warren would be my first "name" opponent and the first true representative of the philosophical tradition that I found so oppressive, not to say intellectually bankrupt, as a graduate student at Berkeley. Its major ingredients were materialism, utilitarianism, and a cryptic descendent of that philosophical worship of science known as logical positivism. And a number of my fellow faculty members from the University would be there. These were the people I saw daily, and now they would be judging my performance.

Because I'm the only one of my colleagues here on campus who speaks in public against abortion, not to mention taking the unpopular side of other controversial topics, I often feel, as I said in the preface, like Don

Quixote – solitary and comical. Although I've always prided myself on my indifference to what people think of me for my positions, on this particular evening I was worrying about what kind of impression I'd make on my colleagues. I reminded myself for the umpteenth time: "Being afraid is the price you pay for speaking out, especially on a hot-button issue like abortion. It was, after all, my freedom to come here this evening. I could've declined the invitation to debate in the first place. The fact is I didn't. So suck it up and get on with it."

Was my fear visible? Maybe not so that you could tell I was afraid. But it apparently produced a noticeable difference in my manner. While walking to McLaren Hall, I met the wife of a good friend and colleague. We exchanged the usual "hello" and "how are you"; I don't recall what else we said to each other during those few seconds. What I do know is that the next day her husband told me: "Mary said she bumped into you last night before the debate and you were higher than a kite." That would have been the adrenaline pumping through my body.

McLaren was packed to the rafters. There must have been a thousand people there waiting for the event to begin. And right in my path stood Scriven talking to a student. I greeted him and we had a congenial few words before I proceeded to the foot of the stage where the student body president who had organized the event and would serve as its moderator was standing. He greeted me and led me over to where Mary Ann Warren was sitting to introduce us to each other. She was a short, slight woman with an attractive, intelligent face. There was no doubt that she wanted the world to know that she was a hard-line, no nonsense feminist. It would be an understatement to say that she wore her feminism on her sleeve. It was her entire wardrobe. She dressed down outrageously: working man's shirt, corduroy pants, workman's high-top brown shoes. No make-up, of course.

The student led us up several stairs to the stage where there were two podiums, each with a microphone, and chair in the background. I can still see the ocean of people sitting before us. I remember trying to calm myself with slow, diaphragmatic breathing. He reminded us of the format: each speaker would have fifteen minutes for presentation, five minutes for rebuttal, and then a couple of minutes to reply to the rebuttal before the moderator asked prepared questions of us. The rest of the time would be spent fielding questions from the audience. It was agreed I would go first.

I'd prepared weeks in advance to answer Warren's argument and had worked out what I thought was a powerful counter-argument. I decided (hoped) that it would be more persuasive if I led up to it by portraying the unborn as a disfavored group of human beings. I used no notes. And despite my jitters leading up to the debate, I found myself speaking confidently and articulately with a strong voice. (I've long been a believer in self-hypnosis or, to use a metaphor from the computer age, self-programming. I forged my presentation over and over, anticipating objections to it and trying to make it as trenchant as possible; over and over I rehearsed it in my mind while driving, walking, alone in my office or study.)

I began by referring to a celebrated court decision in Los Angeles that occurred recently enough to be fresh in the minds of many of the audience. The jury found the defendant guilty of murder in the first degree and the judge sentenced him to death in the gas chamber at San Quentin prison. I pointed out that that decision would automatically go to the court of appeals where three judges would pour over every line of the lower court's transcript to ensure that the defendant's rights had not been violated. But, I continued, we allow no right of review for the unborn, even though he or she has been given a death sentence; abortion, after all, is killing and killing is punishment. Punishment for what? By my tone of voice and stance, I emphatically drove home the grotesqueness of our inconsistency. We demand that a convicted murderer have his case reviewed by a panel of three judges, while at the same time we allow countless unborn human beings to be given the same punishment, death, even though innocent of any crime, without any hearing, let alone any judicial review.

Then it was Warren's turn. Seeing my opponent in action made me feel more confident about my choice of tactic. She was not a strong presence, especially before so large an audience. Mild mannered, she put on thick-lense glasses, and in a soft voice read every line of her argument from a typed manuscript. The major flaw in this facedown method is that the speaker doesn't make any eye contact with the audience. That's all right if your audience is composed of scholars and academics who pride themselves on being interested only in the presentation and on their ability to follow a closely reasoned argument. But it is lethal before an audience of undergraduates and people from the community at large. If they don't see much of your facial expression, gestures and gaze, they find it hard to maintain attention and are apt to form the impression that your argument is weak and that you're losing the debate.

Her argument was just what I expected – it followed her article to a "T." She began by saying that she would agree with my claim that the fetus was an unjustifiably disfavored class of humanity, if it were a person. She defended a woman's moral right to abortion by contending that the fetus was only a potential person. A woman was morally justified in aborting because she was an actual person and the rights of an actual person over-rode the rights of a merely potential person. Warren didn't deny that the fetus was a human being. It had, she said, "genetic humanity" but lacked "moral humanity," to wit, personhood. Thus it was not yet a member of the "moral community."

Her criteria for being a person she took to be "intuitively obvious": consciousness of objects, both internal and external, especially the capacity to feel pain; reasoning; self-motivated activity; the capacity to communicate; the presence of self-concepts and self-awareness.

I don't remember criticizing Warren's distinction between genetic humanity and moral humanity during my five-minute rebuttal. I do remember advancing it in my response to her statement that she would agree with my point if the fetus were a person. In answer to that I challenged her idea of what it takes to be a person as anything but "intuitively obvious," as she said. I insisted that it surely didn't match our experience of human beings. Her idea of what a person *is* made us into pure intellects. But while agreeing that intellect and self-awareness are our most important faculties, I emphasized that our essential being is composed also of feeling and sensation. Experience testifies that we have no knowledge and perform no rational activities that are unaccompanied by sensations, images and feelings, and vice versa. Our essence, our defining characteristic, is not rationality; we are not minds trapped in bodies, as the philosopher, Descartes, claimed. Our defining characteristic is "rational animality," as Aristotle claimed. So the fact that the unborn shows no signs of rational activity doesn't allow us to infer that it is a kind of sub-person. All it shows is that its natural potential for rational activity has not yet been actualized.

One thing about our exchange with the audience made a lasting impression on me. Shortly after Warren's article appeared, some reviewers pointed out that, according to her criteria for personhood, newborn infants aren't persons. This point came up in her reply to a question from a young woman sitting a few rows from the stage. I could see the combined expressions of shock and disapproval on her face when Warren said to her that she didn't think an infant became a person until about nine months after birth. Because the young woman made it clear in her question that she favored abortion, her facial reaction intrigued me. Warren was trying to be consistent with her claim that personhood requires meeting the aforementioned criteria. I couldn't help wondering if the woman, completely innocent of her inconsistency, liked the idea of abortion but not the idea of babies being sub-persons. In other words, unborn babies are not persons because abortion is a quick fix; infants are persons because they're cute and cuddly.

For me, the debate was an important self-test. Although my presentation lacked the cutting edge that it would acquire later on, it nevertheless proved to me that I could hold my own against a major voice for the pro-abortion side. I found out that neither the presence of Michael Scriven nor the opposition of Mary Ann Warren nor a large room filled with people – including my colleagues, some of whom doubtless thought my anti-abortion stance was absurd – could cow me. I couldn't help thinking, "Ma was right; I am a good speaker." That evening I received what was perhaps the best compliment of all. The late Father James Dempsey, S.J., who taught speech and ran the debate team, said to me: "Ray, the good thing about you as a debater is that you don't take any garbage."

The second part of the event, when we answered questions from the audience, brought home to me several things I'd already sensed from my previous speaking experiences. For one thing, what works best for me is replying, not presenting. My finest moments when arguing a point occur not in my presentation but in my responses to questions and comments. Although preparation is absolutely crucial to a successful performance, the fact is I'm one of those people who are more effective when giving spontaneous replies than when delivering prepared presentations. If I were a boxer, I think I'd be known as a counter-puncher. The second thing is that the question period may well be the more important part of the debate. Your responses give you the chance to introduce important points that you didn't bring out in your presentation and to answer criticisms of your position raised by your opponent. You can usually cast your response in such a way as to answer the question and still finish by bringing up such things. The third thing is that the primary object of the debate is not so much convincing your opponent but to use your opponent to get to your audience, to command their attention so that they are receptive to your position and the reasons you advance on its behalf.

I must say that it was a pleasure to debate Mary Ann Warren. We debated each other once more, about ten years later, and appeared on the same panel on a local television show discussing fetal transplants around the same time. Although we stand in sharp disagreement on abortion, she offers a reasoned, straightforward argument in favor of abortion that is directed to the minds of her audience rather than to their emotions. She does not stoop to tricks, manipulations, theatrics or appeals to pity. I mention all this because, looking back on all my debate opponents since her, she was the best. True, she was not a commanding presence at the podium; but she brought with her a professional integrity and intellectual rigor that kept her argument on point throughout. At the time of our first debate, I had no idea that she would be my first and last opponent of substance. (See the Appendix A for another viewpoint of the same debate.)

YOU NEVER KNOW WHOM YOU'RE GOING TO REACH

Despite the mixed results of my foray into the public discourse on abortion, I'd learned a lesson early on that kept my hopes up that the pro-life cause had a good chance of winning. It was 1972. I was doing some teaching at a local community college, where my assignment there was one course in ethics and one in "Patterns of Religion." I discussed abortion in the ethics class but not in the religion class because the latter's structure did not seem to lend itself to ethical considerations. In that class sat a couple who, by their manner of dress and speech, qualified as "hippies" or "counter-culture." Although married, neither wore a wedding band because it was a "sign of chattel-slavery"; when I referred to the woman in class as "Mrs.____," she instructed me in curt tones to address her thereafter as "Ms.____." Towards the end of the semester, they approached me one evening after class with the following story: "Three months ago," she related, "I found out that I was pregnant and we decided that I would get an abortion. But then two of my girl friends who are in your ethics class told us what you said about abortion, so we decided to have the baby." Of all the people in that classroom, I'd have judged them the least likely to accept an anti-abortion argument.

Experiences like that led me to realize that there are a lot of people who are receptive to the anti-abortion argument. Even when they disagree with it, it still gets through to them; they go away thinking about it, and for a simple reason: the intellect turns toward truth just as spontaneously as the eye turns toward light and the ear toward sound. The trouble is that the eye can't turn toward the light if the light's blocked and the intellect can't turn toward the truth if its not presented.

Unfortunately, the pro-abortion people know how to keep the light of truth turned off or at least how to create distractions so that we're not aware that it's on. Lack of understanding, dogmatism, and defensiveness are difficult enough obstacles to surmount. But when you add evasion and manipulation of language and emotion, you erect an obstacle tall enough to block the light, at least temporally. Here's an example.

"PRE-OWNED" SOUNDS BETTER THAN "USED" AND "TERMINATING PREGNANCY" SOUNDS BETTER THAN "KILLING THE UNBORN."

A while back I noticed that car dealers were using a new kind of sign; it read, "Pre-owned Cars." Like the dinosaurs, the sign, "Used Cars," had mysteriously become extinct. That discovery inspired a fantasy in which I approach the car salesman and say: "'Pre-owned cars' is an ambiguous term. It can refer to an automobile that someone owned but never drove or to an automobile that someone not only owned but also drove. Since it makes a huge difference whether the product offered for sale was used by the previous owner, why don't you make two kinds of signs, 'Pre-owned But Never Driven' and 'Pre-owned and Driven'?" Then, pointing to the sky blue, four-door Mercedes Benz majestically occupying a high-lighted portion of the showroom floor, I ask him in a tone of voice exuding all the confidence of a district attorney cocksure that the defense's star witness is about to expose his lack of credibility to the jury, " To which category does this car belong?"

Even in the regions of fantasy, I find it difficult to picture the salesperson pursuing that conversation with me. What are the odds of a "pre-owned car" in a car lot never having been driven by its previous owner? The idea, of course, is that "pre-owned" sounds better than "used." It acknowledges that the car is not new, that it had a previous owner, without focusing attention on the fact that it is used, that it was driven about the town or the state or maybe even the whole United States by its previous owner. In short, "pre-owned" is a euphemism. You intentionally choose a word that is broad enough to refer by inclusion to what you are in fact doing or saying but so broad as not to make specific reference to it.

"Terminating pregnancy" is a euphemism also. The term extends to more things than abortion. When a physician purposely delivers a baby before it is due, he or she is terminating the pregnancy. Physician-induced premature births are done when the woman suffers from pre-eclampsia or some defect of her heart or liver. When this is done, we do not say that the physician "aborted the baby." Because the strict meaning of "abortion" is the "expulsion of a nonviable fetus," the medical profession in the last century placed premature births in the category of "abortion." But nowadays "abortion" means a procedure that aims, as means or end, to kill the fetus. So abortion is a termination of pregnancy, but the way it terminates pregnancy is by killing the unborn. As a broad term, "termination of pregnancy" diverts attention from the grisly reality of abortion. The next time you hear a pro-abortionist or the media say "termination of pregnancy," just remember what you're getting when you buy a "pre-owned car."

When I first got into the public debate on abortion in 1967, it didn't take me long to realize that most of my anti-abortion energies would be spent popping the euphemisms to which the pro-abortionists clung like so many brightly colored balloons at a county fair. True enough, they seemed to have all the weapons they needed to succeed in their mission to liberalize the abortion laws. Besides winning liberal support by casting it in images of personal freedom and women's reproductive rights, they succeeded in persuading the public that the laws restricting abortion needed to be abandoned. No doubt a large part of their success in molding popular opinion came from inflated claims about the number of illegal, back alley abortions performed annually in the United States. They'd managed to get the lawmakers, the judges, and the media on their side.

But if their weapons were daunting, their armor was paper-thin. It was

clear from the outset that what the pro-abortionists feared most was having their euphemisms exposed, having public attention focused on what
terms like "fetus," "reproductive freedom," "termination of pregnancy,"
"removing the fetal parts," and even "abortion" were all about – the deliberate killing of unborn children. The only thing is that, just as in war-
fare, where you can't penetrate your enemy's defenses without getting to
the right positions with the right weapons and with the soldiers who are
willing to use them, so we wouldn't be able to expose the claims and
arguments of the pro-abortionists for what they really were – word-games
and factual distortions – without confronting them in public debate.

CHAPTER TWO

FIGHTING SMOG WITH A CROWBAR

"I must say, Sir Carrasco, that we have what we deserve....Don Quixote's mad, we're sane. He goes off fit and smiling while your lordship is left battered and cheerless. Let's inquire, then, who's the madder: the one who's mad because he can't help it or the one who's mad by free choice?"

The Adventures of Don Quixote, Part II, Ch. XV

Until 1967 my involvement with the abortion issue was confined to discussions with university colleagues and classroom presentations in my ethics courses. But even at that it was a relatively recent topic of interest. Like most hot social issues, the abortion controversy didn't just explode on the social scene without warning. It simmered for a few years, gradually heating up before bursting onto the public scene. Starting in the late 1950s, the media carried reports about this or that woman trying to get an abortion. Then in 1961, we had the thalidomide horror. During the previous year, physicians began prescribing the drug on a regular basis for pregnant women suffering nausea. The discovery that the drug caused severe birth deformities came too late. Many babies were born without hands or feet, some even without arms or legs. Shirley Finkbine became a celebrated thalidomide case. Fearing that the thalidomide her doctor had prescribed might have deformed her unborn child, she unsuccessfully appealed all the way to the Arizona State Supreme Court to be allowed an abortion. She finally went to Sweden for the abortion.

Not surprisingly, the abortion issue started surfacing in ethics classes when I was an undergraduate as well as in the ethics classes I would teach later on. I remember one of my students asking, "What about a woman who has four children already and is told by her doctors that she'll die or lose her leg if she carries the pregnancy to term?" Her question was indicative; it was always the hardship cases that were presented. For example, I remember one episode on a prime time television series in the early sixties, called "The Doctors and the Nurses." A pregnant mother of five children, who was admitted to the hospital for some ailment or other, told her physician that she wanted an abortion. It seems her husband, although a loving, attentive father, was a very poor provider; he couldn't hold a job. The hospital refused her request and all three of the hospital's chaplains – Catholic, Protestant, and Jew – made it plain they couldn't condone it either. But the pro-abortion message came across nonetheless. Not only was she depicted as a sympathetic character, not only was she pleading a hardship case, but more significantly, the television program was proposing abortion as a humane possibility rather than an unspeakable act.

It is hard to imagine a more powerful influence on the public consciousness than television. I don't mean to say that the television industry was the source and center of the pro-abortion movement; that lay somewhere else. But television is an enormously powerful instrument of propaganda. As Marshall McCluhan observed in *The Mechanical Bride*, the superiority of video for propaganda is that it presents the viewer with an image before he has time to form his own. Owing to its capacity to tell stories with pictures, television probably contributed more than any other agency to the public acceptance of abortion. There is no better way of shaping mass culture than to veil biased ethical and political viewpoints in the clothes of entertainment and human interest. That is exactly what television is doing today to sell physician-assisted suicide and homosexuality.

FINESSED BY POLITICIANS

Then, too, there was the mounting pressure on legislators – from feminist organizations and the pro-abortion lobby – for the reform of existing abortion laws. In 1967 Alan Beilenson – then a California state senator from Beverly Hills and now a congressman – introduced the "Therapeutic Abortion Law" to the legislature in Sacramento. Legal abortions were not easy to get in those days in the United States, as was clear in the Shirley Finkbine case. Beilenson's bill would allow a woman a legal abortion if: (1) the pregnancy were due to rape or incest; (2) she had contracted German measles in the first trimester of pregnancy; (3) carrying the baby to term would injure her physical health; (4) carrying it to term would injure her mental health. If passed into law, California would be the second state to liberalize its abortion law. New York had done so in 1966.

I sent a four-page single spaced typed letter to my elected officials in Sacramento, setting forth reasons why they should vote against Beilenson's bill. Notice the lack of any mention of whether abortion kills human beings in State Senator Alfred E. Alquist's reply:

> April 13, 1967
>
> Thank you for your most thoughtful analysis of the pragmatic and moral questions involved in legalized abortion, and the conclusions, which lead you to oppose the Beilenson Bill.
>
> The question confronting the Legislature, however, is not one of being for or against abortion. The basic question is how effective are our present laws. Statistics indicate over ten thousand illegal abortions annually in the United States, with over a third of our maternity deaths due to this cause.
>
> Adequate safeguards are written into the Beilenson Bill, and it has the endorsement of the California Medical Association.

State Senator Clark L. Bradley makes the same omission in his reply:

April 20, 1967

Thank you for your recent letter and very comprehensive analysis of the pending legislation on abortion and your general position on the subject.

I am sure that we would agree that we are discussing a very fundamental matter in which there are two distinct schools of thought.

I appreciate your very learned and well-presented presentation of your point of view on this matter.

Busloads of us, from anti-abortion groups and churches in the San Francisco Bay Area, went to the state capital to sit in at the Senate Judiciary Committee's public hearing of the bill. The committee heard the pro and con arguments from a number of "experts." Being there gave me an appreciation for the intelligence of politicians.

For example, a physician testified that without a law such as Beilenson proposed, the state would have to spend more money on newborn patients. One of the Judiciary Committee asked, "How much more, in dollars and cents, would it cost?" The physician replied, "About twenty-five dollars for each patient." What impressed me about the question was that its demand for a specific sum of money prevented the audience and the committee from assuming, as we are likely to do when it comes to government spending, that the prediction of "increased costs" would be huge. The committee member's question deprived the physician's argument of any persuasive force.

Beilenson was pretty sharp, too. Testifying against the bill was a researcher from the aerospace industry. At one point, Beilenson asked him in what area he had his Ph.D. "Engineering," he replied. "Have you taken any courses in biology?," Beilenson continued. The witness admitted he hadn't. That was a damning admission coming from someone who represented himself as a scientist speaking on behalf of the unborn. An attorney as well as a politician, Beilenson knew the importance of researching witnesses for their weak points before getting them on the witness stand.

Then there was a soft-spoken witness against the bill, a physician from Visalia. He brilliantly exploded Beilenson's basis for arguing that the state needs his therapeutic abortion law. Beilenson claimed that a reported 500,000 illegal abortions took place annually in the United States. To this, the witness replied that, given the National Health Association's claim that only 250 maternal deaths were reported in the previous year in this country, we would have to infer that illegal abortions were safer than giving birth since, out of 500,000 illegal abortions, hospitals should have records of more deaths than that. Beilenson quickly parried, "The deaths aren't reported." Just as quickly the witness emphasized that we were talking here about dead adult females; where, he asked, are all the bodies?

The physician also scored points by saying that he was a "family physician," a field, he noted, which gave him unrivaled opportunities to observe the long term effects on women who have had abortions – he saw them not only when they were girls but in adulthood and middle age as well. The physician performing the abortion, on the other hand, sees them only for the abortion and sometimes for a follow-up shortly after and thus is in no position to pronounce on the long term physical or psychological effects of the procedure.

At the end of the day, it was clear that the anti-abortion side had given better reasons against the bill than the other side had given for it. In our innocence of things political, we had hoped that the committee would then reject Beilenson's bill; instead they voted to table it. I suspect this is what politicians do when they wish to avoid criticism or outcry from one side or the other in the audience.

At all events, in 1968 the Legislature voted the bill into law. Immediately the number of legal abortions performed in the state rose like a rocket. Not surprisingly, over ninety percent of them were done to "protect the woman's mental health." This is how it worked: the psychiatrist would sign his name to a document claiming that, in his judgment, the woman would do violence to herself or to her baby if forced to carry it to term. The ink was hardly dry on the new law when the main editorial of the *Oakland Tribune* praised the law because it promised to save the state huge amounts of money in welfare payments. The editorial noted that, whereas the state then paid a welfare mother $150 a month per child until he or she was eighteen years of age, an abortion would be a one time cost to the state of no more than $250.

"UNITED FOR LIFE"

By 1968 I had unwittingly assumed the mantle of the anti-abortion spokes-person at the University of Santa Clara. Every time a request from the community at large came in for someone to give the Catholic Church's position on abortion, I was summoned. At first it was for presentations before this or that church group and occasionally at business or profes-sional groups' breakfast or luncheon meetings with the usual questions and comments following. (I still have a gilt-covered ruler bearing the Kiwanis Club's logo given me by its Santa Clara chapter for speaking at one of those breakfast talks.)

In 1970, I got "my big break." That was the appearance on the "Joe Dolan" radio show that I described in Chapter One. It would be the first of my radio and television appearances on which I spoke against abortion or euthanasia.

That same year, a group in San Francisco led by Frank Filice, who was then a professor of biology at the University of San Francisco, founded a pro-life organization called "United for Life." Its aim was educational rather than political, and it was composed primarily of academics, a sprin-kling of housewives and business people, with a couple of attorneys and physicians also on the roster. I'd already made up my mind not to join until, one evening, I got a phone call from someone who heard me on the radio. He sounded as if he had interesting things to say about the abortion issue, so I invited him to our home.

He had come from Italy about ten years previously and since then worked as a gardener. He was in the habit of listening to talk shows on his portable radio while doing his gardening and that's how he heard me speak on abortion. He encouraged me to join "United for Life" despite the appearance of overwhelming odds against the anti-abortion move-ment. With his accent, small stature, mustache and wavy dark, graying hair, he reminded me of the popular 1940s movie actor, J. Carroll Nash, who frequently played the role of an Italian peasant or Spanish guerrilla freedom fighter. In his Italian accent, he told me that I must join United For Life so that when future generations studied our era, they would see that we took an organized stand against abortion. I remember the sense of being part of a B movie drama that evening. How could I resist? He made me feel like a reluctant civilian who knew that in the end he must drop his plow (books, in my case) and come to the defense of the cause. True, I was already speaking frequently in public against abortion, but joining "United for Life" put me in a community of like-minded people from whom I learned and drew inspiration. After all these years, I still have a copy of our brochure, and a classy one it is. Not only did we take pains in making sure of the wording of our statement of purpose, but also the cover had Leonardo da Vinci's sketch of the child in the womb. I don't remember the gardener's name, but I'm forever in his debt.

Shortly afterwards, a group of us formed United for Life of Santa Clara. We had no affiliation with "United for Life" in San Francisco, but we did share its ethos since our goals and activities were educational rather than political. The president was a low-key guy who worked in the computer industry in Silicon Valley. He described himself as a political and economic conservative and confessed, without embarrassment, that he'd flunked out of college twice. He and his wife were Protestants, which was unusual in my Catholic anti-abortion circles, but that had no bearing on our work together in the group.

We held monthly meetings, usually in church halls and a couple of times I got us an empty classroom at the University of Santa Clara. We tried to have a speaker each time with the business meeting afterwards. We put out a newsletter for our members and filled requests for anti-abortion speakers. Abortion was more of a hotly contested topic then than it is today. Besides Doug Harper, a psychiatrist, Bob Kelley, a physician and myself, the rest of the active membership consisted entirely of nonprofessionals. We did have the support of priests, ministers, and some other physicians. A children's dentist and an activist physician attended a few of our meeting in the beginning.

The activist physician was a Mormon. He came to a couple of our early meetings, but that was all. I suspect he was too much the activist to find a home with our purely educational purposes. At one meeting, he urged the group to have a camp-out on the front lawn of Good Samaritan Hospital in San Jose to protest their abortion practices. I recall his words: "With a name like that, they shouldn't be doing what they're doing." Another time, when we joined other pro-life groups in San Francisco to picket a meeting of the San Francisco Medical Association, he appeared in the picket line, holding high for all to see, a clear plastic bag containing very bloody contents. He announced that he had just removed them from a woman's uterus that morning and that it was what an abortion's aftermath looked like. He certainly would never do an abortion, so I had no idea what the contents were.

The president preferred to work in the background and have me up front as the group's representative. For example, we co-sponsored, with a local hospital, a luncheon talk by the distinguished Dr. Albert Liley. He was a perinatologist from New Zealand who gained prominence as the first one to successfully give a blood transfusion to a child in the womb. An outspoken opponent of abortion, we were thrilled to have a physician of his international renown on our side, despite the fact that he favored abortion in cases of rape. His presentation, with slides, argued that the unborn should be treated as a little patient with its own life, even to the point of taking charge of determining when it will start its journey down the uterine canal toward daylight. I remember reading in one of his books a report that a pregnant woman who'd had oxygen pumped into her uterus for some medical reason or other complained that when she lay down at night – apparently the oxygen bubble then engulfed the baby's head – the baby's crying kept her husband and her awake all night. I'm just reporting what he wrote. Anyway, at the president's request, I presided over the luncheon, introduced Dr. Liley, and directed questions and comments from the audience to him. It's hard to describe the inspiration and sense of support that comes from listening to an eminent physician and medical researcher speak against abortion by sharing his medical research on the life of the baby in the womb.

THE THREAT FROM THE OVERPOPULATION LOBBY

The movement for liberalized abortion laws got considerable momentum from population control advocates and that portion of the public they were able to influence through the media. The 1960s and 1970s were decades of panic among many intellectuals and professionals in the United States over the perception that Third World couples were having too many children, a situation which, if allowed to continue, would inevitably lead to overpopulation and global disaster. Books like Paul Ehrlich's, *The Population Bomb*, and Garrett Hardin's *Exploring New Ethics for Survival* along with his essay, "The Tragedy of the Commons," were widely read and influential. The advocacy group, "Zero Population Growth," headquartered in the beautiful and upscale Los Altos Hills area, about 35 miles south of San Francisco, maintained that each couple in the United States should limit themselves to two children. "ZPG" and other such groups not only advocated contraception for the Third World but saw abortion and sterilization as necessary backstops to a successful population control program. Thus, Hardin wrote: "No single method of birth control is foolproof, but there can be a perfect *system* of birth control. All that is necessary is that elective abortion be included in the set of methods used – as a back-up method, when other methods fail (for whatever reason)." Both Ehrlich and Hardin toyed with the proposals by some writers for universal sterilization policies. For example: the government would put sterilants in our drinking water. Any couple wanting a second child would have to secure government approval; they would then present proof of approval to their physician who, in turn, would write them a prescription for an antidote to the sterilant. On Johnny Carson's "Tonight Show," Erhlich pointed with obvious pride to a pin in his lapel, which, he proclaimed, indicated that he'd had a vasectomy. That, we were to believe, was the patriotic, humanitarian, and noble thing to do.

On one occasion, a member of our biology department and I engaged in a civilized argument at lunch in the faculty club over the need for population control here in the United States. To my remark that my four children were no burden to society because my wife and I took responsibility for their upbringing – food, shelter, education, etc. – she replied that four were still too many children for a family because the six of us were using up some of her oxygen! To give an idea of how pervasive was the social pressure for limiting family size, I recall a married woman at the time who was carrying her fourth child telling me that being pregnant again made her feel "dirty." My impression was that many women felt that way.

What frightened the population control crowd was not only the prospect of overcrowding or the planet's inability to feed a burgeoning humanity but the depletion of natural resources and the pollution of our atmosphere and drinking water. In a public, dramatic gesture of resistance to the occurrence of these calamities, the San Jose State University student body buried a Ford Mustang, with media present, of course, to show their repudiation of fuel-guzzling, air-polluting automobiles from Detroit.

By 1970 the population panic was apparently great enough to inspire at least one medical journal to see it as a catalyst for rethinking the traditional theory of the right to life. In a remarkable editorial entitled, "A New Ethic for Medicine and Society," in *The Journal of California Medicine* (now called *The Journal of Western Medicine*), the editor took the position that the Judeo-Christian ethic, particularly that portion of it which demands equal reverence for every human life, is decaying. The causes of this decay, the piece continued, were (1) public concern over uncontrolled population growth and the apparent incapacity of available resources "to support these numbers in the manner in which they are or would like to become accustomed" and (2) "a quite new social emphasis on something which is beginning to be called the quality of life, a something which becomes possible (*sic*) for the first time in human history because of scientific and technologic development." How far the decay of the traditional Judeo-Christian ethic has gone can be seen, the editorial proceeded, in the current widespread practice of abortion insofar as abortion is clearly the killing of a human being.

Acknowledging the pervasive influence exerted till now by the traditional ethic upon Western society, and specifically on the practice of medicine, the editor urged the medical profession to accept the emerging, new ethic, an ethic which assigns *relative* rather than absolute value to human life, in anticipation of the inevitable extension from the problems of birth control and birth selection to the problems of death control and death selection.

Understandably, population control advocates and anti-abortionists saw each other as mortal enemies. I got, what I believe, was a personal taste of the former's animus toward us. One springtime in the early 1970s, I accepted an invitation from the local chapter of the Sierra Club, a powerful lobbying force for environmental protection on the state and Federal levels, to lecture at their fall meeting. My proposed topic was "The Natural Environment, Population, and the Dignity of Persons." After several months passed without any follow up from them, I called for confirmation. I'd reached the woman who had originally invited me, and she gave reassurances that everything was on and that they were looking forward to hearing me speak. At the time, I found her reassurances anything but reassuring: her speech seemed strained and she herself seemed nervous and tentative. When fall came, she called me to tell me that they wouldn't need my services. I have a vague recollection that she gave as the reason that some members of the Sierra Club objected to having me speak. I'm almost sure that it wasn't until after they invited me that they found out that I was an anti-abortionist.

Not surprisingly, then, it was common, when speaking against abortion, to have someone in the audience justify the necessity of the procedure by appealing to the urgency of stemming the mounting tide of world population. What struck me about this argument is its complete lack of concern for the human beings who would be slaughtered. It would be one thing if supporters of this proposed remedy had reached the conclusion that the unborn were not human beings or persons. I know that conclusion would be mistaken, but at least their argument would not rest on a willingness to kill countless innocent and helpless human beings. My own impression was that the status of the unborn victims was simply not a concern for them: human beings or not, their sacrifice was necessary for the survival of the human species. That inspired me to publish a reply – my first article ever! – entitled "The Papal Encyclicals and the 'Population Bomb'" in the *Social Justice Review.*

Accordingly, many of our presentations attacked the theories of runaway population growth. For example, at one of our local anti-abortion meetings, we got a physicist from the University of Santa Clara to present a paper in which he argued that the earth could comfortably support 15 billion human beings. He based this claim on two requirements: the mastery of nuclear fusion to replace nuclear fission, thereby furnishing us with a virtually limitless supply of nonpolluting energy – "little suns," he called them – and the production of subway type vehicles directed toward the earth's center. This would save fuel by using the pull of gravity from the center to pull these vehicles to "airplane speeds." What this would allow, he said, was for large populations to live out in the vast and currently unpopulated areas of our country and still be able to get to and from work in the major cities in a reasonable time.

MORE FINESSING BY POLITICIANS

In October, 1972, I even wrote a letter of complaint to the Committee on Human Rights at the United Nations, calling their attention to the legal wholesale abortions taking place in the United States, insofar as these violated its declaration on the rights of the unborn:

> The child, by reason of his physical and mental immaturity, needs special safeguards and care, including appropriate legal protection, *before as well as after birth*.

> The child shall enjoy special protection, and shall be given opportunities and facilities, by law and by other means, to enable him to develop physically, mentally, morally, spiritually and socially in a healthy and normal manner and in conditions of freedom and dignity. *In the enactment of laws for this purpose the best interests of the child shall be the paramount considerations*. (My emphases)

This last statement of the declaration was, and is, especially relevant to the abortions in the United States because one of the major arguments the feminists have always used to justify "abortion on request" was "reproductive freedom." The aim of this freedom was to liberate women from the social constraints of motherhood so that they could become the economic and social equals of men. Several weeks later, I received the following reply from the Secretary of the United Nations Human Rights Committee: "The Human Rights Committee has instructed me to inform you that they have read your letter with interest."

From the very start, we were pessimistic about the chances of reversing the tide to legalize abortion. But our most demoralizing setback came in 1973 with the U.S. Supreme Court's *Roe v. Wade* decision. Until then, anti-abortion groups in other parts of the country weren't doing badly. Liberal California proved a hard sell for the pro-life message, even with its large conservative voting bloc in Orange County. So too did Oregon, whose citizens voted liberal abortion into law. But voters in Michigan and North Dakota rejected pro-abortion legislation by 2 to 1 and 3 to 1, respectively. Until the court's decision, it looked as if we were finally making some headway.

The pro-life groups and churches exhorted us to send letters to the members of the U.S. Supreme Court to protest their decision. I wrote letters of support to those Justices who dissented from the majority opinion and letters of criticism to those that signed on to it. I don't think I got any replies. We were also exhorted to write our representatives in the nation's capitol, urging them to support an anti-abortion amendment to the Constitution. Given the implausibility of the high court reversing itself on *Roe v. Wade*, a Constitutional amendment seemed our only hope.

On January 20, 1974, I sent practically identical letters to Congressman Don Edwards and U.S. Senator Alan Cranston. The 2nd and 3rd paragraphs were only in the letter to Cranston, as he had been a correspondent in pre-World War II Germany, providing the first English translation of Hitler's *Mein Kampf* for the American people. I'd hope to get his attention by referring to the Nazi's "crimes against humanity."

Dear....

With the approaching anniversary of the U.S. Supreme Court's decision on abortion, I should like to take this opportunity to encourage your support for one of the pro-life amendments, whether Hogan's or Buckley's, etc., now under consideration by the Congress.

In my judgment, the wholesale abortions now in progress signal the most serious of threats to the dignity and freedom of the person and, hence, to free society. I say this in the light of our scientific knowledge, which, for any open-minded person, raises the question, "Is induced abortion the deliberate killing of a human being?" It is an unavoidable conclusion that any society that looks to liberalized abortion for the solution to its problems is well on the way to losing its respect for human life. And, since the right to life is the most fundamental of all rights, it follows that a society which no longer feels constrained to respect that right is certainly under no constraint to respect the other rights, such as free speech, etc.

With your direct experience of pre-World War II Germany, I need not remind you of the climate of death dealing which preceded Hitler's rise to power. Grünberger points out in his history of the Third Reich that there were in pre-1933 Germany between 600,000 and 800,000 abortions annually as opposed to between one million and a million-and-one quarter births.

Would it not be a monstrous irony if the United States should embark upon the same programs of exterminating the "unfit" and "unwanted" for which it enjoined in the prosecution of the Nazis for the "crimes against humanity"?

I hope and pray...that you will see your way clear to support the pro-life amendment, which in your judgment is the most reasonable.

Sincerely yours,

[signed] Raymond Dennehy

On March 29, 1974, Congressman Edwards replied:

Dear Mr. Dennehy,

I have received your sincere and earnest letter urging congressional action on H.J. Res. 261, Congressman's Hogan's proposal to amend the United States Constitution and outlaw abortions. I have read your letter with respect and want to thank you for describing your very real concern in this matter.

Many who have written me on this subject also mention that I have not stated my personal view on abortion. This is true, my reason being that as Chairman of the Judiciary Sub-committee handling the legislation, I think it would not be appropriate for me to judge the issue before the evidence is in. This is also my position on the impeachment inquiry concerning President Nixon.

There is obviously considerable misunderstanding regarding my power as Chairman of the Civil Rights and Constitutional Rights Subcommittee of the House Committee on the Judiciary. Priorities for hearings in all House Committees and Subcommittees are established by a majority of the Committee and Subcommittee members, and the rights of the majority to establish priorities must be respected by the Chairman.

In addition to the Hogan bill, 602 bills proposed by other House Members, including 107 legislative proposals for constitutional amendments on many subjects, have been referred to the Subcommittee I chair. Included, for example, are 49 bills to amend the Constitution on busing and a total of 28 on abortion. The abortion amendments vary from the Hogan proposal, which would outlaw abortion, to H.R. 254, which would permit abortion solely on the application of the woman. We also have a number of proposed constitutional amendments relating to presidential and congressional tenure.

So far the members of my Subcommittee have decided that legislation other than the Hogan amendment shall be considered first. This decision is undoubtedly prompted by the fact that few Members of the House of Representatives have expressed interest in the abortion issue at this time.

As you may know the Senate Judiciary Subcommittee on Constitutional Amendments has held hearings on the subject of abortion on March 6 and 7, 1974. I understand additional hearings are tentatively scheduled for April 11, 1974. In the event you wish to communicate your views to the Senate Subcommittee, you should write to Senator Birch Bayh, Chairman, Senate Office Building, Washington, D.C.

I am naturally quite concerned that certain publications are blaming me personally for holding up the hearings. This is simply not true, and I am writing in hopes of clearing the air. I do appreciate your writing to me and sharing your views on this important issue.

With kindest regards,

Sincerely,

[Signed] Don Edwards

Member of Congress

Cranston wrote his reply on May 23, 1974.

Dear Dr. Dennehy:

Thank you for taking the time to write to me about the January 22, 1973 Supreme Court decision on abortion invalidating under the Constitution state laws that prohibit or restrict a woman in obtaining an abortion during the first three months of pregnancy.

I am deeply concerned by an action that in any way seems to so many people to constitute governmental sanction of the destruction of human life. I am particularly concerned by the social and ethical implications of any such actions now, given the general atmosphere of violence and callousness toward life in our society and in our world.

At the same time, in the case of *Roe, et. Al. v. Bolton, Attorney General of Georgia, et. al,* the Supreme Court based its decision on the Constitution, which is the supreme law of the land. Consequently, the decision cannot be altered or revoked by statute.

In response to the high Court decision, several members of the Congress have proposed resolutions calling for a Constitutional amendment. I am not at present inclined to support such measures. I believe we must approach amendments to the Constitution with the greatest caution and not proceed in the heat of response to a specific unpopular decision of the Court – even though that decision may be one which results in strong controversy and deeply felt emotional and personal objections.

I do not pretend that this is a simple or easily resolved issue. I recognize the very strong beliefs and feelings on both sides. Again, thank you for writing. I welcome, and indeed depend upon different viewpoints on vital issues to broaden my understanding of them.

Sincerely,

[signed] Alan Cranston

On May 29, I replied to the Senator's reply.

Dear Senator Cranston:

Thank you for your reply of May 23 to my letter of January 20. Your expression of deep concern for the "ethical implications" of the Supreme Court's decision of January 22, 1973 is encouraging.

However, I cannot help but wonder how you, as a member of the United State Senate, propose to translate this concern into action. The reasons you give in your letter against presently supporting a Constitutional amendment to protect the right of the unborn to life are ambiguous and misleading. I take the liberty of quoting you:

"I believe we must approach amendments to the Constitution with the greatest caution and not proceed in the heat of response to a specific unpopular decision of the Court – even though that decision may be one which results in strong controversy and deeply felt emotional and personal objection."

To the extent that your words counsel prudence and the exercise of calm judgment, they are beyond all criticism. But your words also seem to imply that such restraint is all the more necessary in the case of a right to life amendment because its primary inspiration is "deeply felt emotional and personal [subjective?] objection." Such an implication excludes from consideration the vast body of scientific evidence, which furnishes *reasoned* and *objective* support for the claim that induced abortion is the direct killing of an unborn child. To be sure, the abortion debate has generated intense emotions; but so did the civil rights and anti-war movements. Yet, as I recall, politicians and journalists did not refer to the pro and con positions as "deeply felt emotional and personal objections." The question of the morality of induced abortion is just as much a question of respect for the rights of the innocent person as are the questions of civil rights and the bombing of civilians.

The evidence from biology and fetology is such as to lead any open-minded person to ask whether induced abortion is the direct killing of an innocent and defenseless human being. I am surprised that you make no mention of this evidence in your letter, but employ instead what seems to be systematically evasive and ambiguous language. The fact that abortion "on request" now has the sanction of the Supreme Court is in itself no more a justification for the morality of it than was the Court's disenfranchisement of blacks in the Dred Scot decision of 1857 a justification for the denial of Constitutional protection for a portion of humanity. It should not be necessary to point out that what is legal is not necessarily what is moral.

You, Senator Cranston, are one of our elected representatives. In that capacity, I believe that, on a matter as grave as induced abortion, you have a serious obligation to your constituents to state *clearly* your position on induced abortion and to reveal in a *forthright manner* what stance you, as a legislator, intend to take in response to the Supreme Court's decision of January 22, 1973. Anything less would be a betrayal of the public trust and an abuse of your office.

Yours sincerely,

[Signed] Raymond Dennehy

It wasn't until October 1 that Cranston finally replied to my reply:

> Dear Dr. Dennehy:
>
> Thank you for your letter sharing further with me your views on abortion. As I indicated previously, I have deep concerns about the implications of the Supreme Court decision, and will continue to consider carefully any material presented to me on this difficult issue.
>
> I welcome the information that you have sent me and trust that although our views are not totally in accord on this matter, it will not affect the agreement that we may have in other areas of mutual concern.
>
> With best wishes,
>
> Sincerely,
>
> [Signed] Alan Cranston

Amidst the darkness of pro-abortion victories, a shining symbol of hope momentarily, but gloriously, illuminated our pro-life aspirations. I don't know if many of today's generation of pro-life people know about Ellen McCormack; it wouldn't surprise me if hardly any of them ever heard of her. This grandmother and wife of a retired New York City police detective had been a career housewife. But when the abortion movement and its anti-life legislation started rolling over the country, she took a gigantic step: she entered politics in the hope of defeating the pro-abortion lobby. First, she made an unsuccessful attempt at the Lt. Governor's seat in Albany. It would be an understatement to say that the defeat failed to discourage her. For in 1976 she ran for the Democratic Party's presidential nomination.

The charge of being a "one-issue candidate" dogged Ellen McCormack throughout her campaign. She took a lot of heat from Democrats as well as from an incredulous but predictably snide liberal media. In every state where she campaigned she won enough support to qualify for matching Federal funds: in Massachusetts she garnered 5% of the Democratic vote,

8% in Wisconsin and 9.4% in the Vermont primary. In the end, Ellen McCormack achieved what she had set out to do. She went to the national convention of the Democratic party in Madison Square Garden in the summer of 1976 with enough delegates to force the party to allow her anti-abortion message to be delivered not only to the convention but to a national television audience as well.

I said above that I didn't think many in today's generation of pro-life advocates had ever heard of Ellen McCormack. Yet her eclipse has a poetic logic about it. Emerging unheralded from the ranks of ordinary folks, she managed to make an extraordinarily powerful statement on behalf of the unborn before quietly returning to the anonymous life of housewife and grandmother.

On January 22, 1977, the fourth anniversary of the United States' Supreme Court's *Roe v. Wade* decision, a friend and I drove to Sacramento to join the pro-life protest, which included visiting some of our elected officials, just to remind them that we're still around as a voting bloc. One of our first stops was at the office of the late State Senator, William Foran. His administrative assistant ushered us, about thirty strong, into Foran's private office. Seated behind his desk, which, under the circumstances he probably regarded as a kind of fortress, he didn't seem happy to see us. I remember his answers to our questions were defensive and even petulant, particularly when he was asked how he would vote on abortion legislation. I remember thinking, at the time, "This guy's our elective representative; he should be giving us clear, courteous answers, but instead he's playing games, even trying to intimidate us."

There was an elderly woman in our doughty little group who may or may not have been intimated by her surroundings, but she had her battle-plan. She stood there, staring unflinchingly at him; with both arms she was holding a large crucifix motionless on the top of her head. Maybe she thought the senator was Count Dracula or one of his vampiric minions. Imagine. A politician who sucks blood from the people and assumes different appearances to avoid getting cornered??? ....Naaah.

I can't remember why I stopped writing our elected representatives and other public officials about abortion. Maybe I just got tired of trying to use reason to persuade politicians to change their position on so controversial and politically dangerous an issue; it proved to be as ineffective as trying to fight smog with a crowbar. Politicians want our votes, but they hardly ever want to tell us where they stand on controversial issues. Despite their clear and serious obligation to clarify their positions, they don't appreciate being pressed to do it. Unless you can scare them with the threat of a recall or loss of office in the next election, they will continue their evasive tactics.

A CLIMATE OF DEATH

Like the supporters of any new movement, we anti-abortionists had boundless enthusiasm for the cause. This is surprising when you consider how many of us were pessimistic about our chances of reversing the momentum of the pro-abortionists. Maybe the enthusiasm was an expression of a primal energy that surfaces from deep within one's being when confronted by a threat to civilization. The threat we perceived was not only from abortion but also from infanticide and euthanasia. Increasingly, we heard stories of newborn babies left untreated and allowed to die in infant intensive care wards because of deformity or retardation. And in 1974 the California legislature passed into law State Senator Barry Keane's natural death bill, which established brain death as constituting legal death. Until then California accepted only the traditional "vital signs" criteria: cessation of independent cardiac and respiratory activity, etc. Many, not just pro-lifers, feared that the brain death test was unreliable and would be used to pronounce people dead when they were really still alive in order to harvest their organs for transplant.

Given this fixation on the perceived climate of death in society, it is easy to understand that some of us would be a bit too quick to interpret reports of newborn deaths in hospitals as unjustifiable euthanasia. I confess to having made that kind of hasty inference once myself. A woman, active in pro-life circles in the San Jose area, told me that the ICU staff at the Kaiser Permanente Hospital in Santa Clara allowed a newborn to die because of various birth defects. The way she described the incident led me to assume that the child was not so grievously afflicted as to justify the refusal to attempt to save it. The next day I brought the incident to the attention of my class and told the students that it was another case of the callous disregard for human life spawned by liberalized abortion.

A woman in the class happened to be a staff worker at that hospital, and she carried my words back to the hospital's ICU. A day later I got a call from one of its physicians. He was, given my harsh interpretation of his decision not to treat the infant, unexpectedly pleasant as he informed me that I'd misrepresented the case. Apparently the newborn weighed about one pound and suffered from kidney failure. I can't recall if his account of things was detailed enough to justify the decision to withhold treatment from the infant in terms of what is called extraordinary or disproportionate means of treatment. I do remember my embarrassment at being so quick to assume that the infant's death was a mercy killing. A professor who teaches medical ethics should be more measured in his responses. I thanked him for taking the time to clarify the case for me and then proceeded feebly to justify my initial reaction to it. You could describe my behavior at that moment as defensive.

I'll be the first to admit that my initial reaction to the case was knee-jerk and unjustifiable. But in fairness, you have to take into account the premises on which our pro-life view of contemporary society was based. First, we were against abortion because we held that the unborn was a human being from the moment of conception. The widespread practice of abortion was nothing less, therefore, than mass murder. Second, it was immediately clear to us that if society could justify killing a human being within the womb, it could not consistently object to killing a human being already born. The beginnings of the drive for legalized euthanasia only verified our fears.

Take, for example, the "Johns Hopkins Hospital Baby" episode, which occurred in 1971. The baby was born with two disorders: Duodenal atresia, which makes it impossible to take food or drink by mouth and Downs's syndrome. The hospital surgeon was confident that the first was easily correctable with standard surgical procedure. But the parents declined to permit the surgery because the baby was retarded. So the hospital placed the baby in a bassinet in a corner of the infant intensive care unit with a sign on it, "Nothing by mouth." After fifteen days the baby died from dehydration. No charges were brought against the parents or the hospital.

A similar case occurred shortly thereafter in Bloomington, Indiana. The parents of a newborn child suffering from Down's syndrome asked the hospital not to feed him. The hospital denied the request and instructed the parents to take the child home. Once at home, the parents refused to feed the child, believing that, because of his retardation, he would be better off dead. Before the child died from starvation, others offered to adopt him, but to no avail. Although the Bloomington District Attorney brought the parents up on charges of "extreme child neglect," the judge refused to try the case.

PRO-LIFE CONVENTIONS

Our California pro-life conventions were well attended and we were lucky to have a number of good speakers and workshops. The first one I attended was in 1969 in Hollywood. At first, going there was out of the question because, trying to support a wife and four small children on a junior professor's salary left no money for non-emergency expenditures. But when the president of our pro-life group informed me that they would like me to attend the convention as United for Life's representative and that they would pay for the plane ticket, hotel, meals, and conference registration fee, I eagerly accepted.

Hundreds of people attended the affair and the speakers filled us with a sense of the imminent threat to democratic life from the pro-abortionists. They exhorted us to intensify our struggle by letting our elected representatives know how we felt about pro-abortion legislation and by forming speakers' bureaus to provide the schools and media with speakers. You could go away from there convinced that Armageddon was at hand.

It was at the convention banquet that I began to understand why Hollywood is called "La La Land." The after dinner speaker was introduced to us as a cosmetic surgeon from the Los Angeles area who was active in civic light opera. He was a youngish man, meticulously dressed, with a neatly trimmed, close-cropped beard. After he got into his talk, it was clear why the light opera part of his resume was mentioned. Having exhorted us to be creative and to explore the different avenues for stemming the tide of pro-abortion legislation, he began to serenade us with two full verses of the song, "Climb Every Mountain." This caught me off guard; I'd never heard anything like that in a talk or speech. While he was singing, I had to look around to see how the others were taking it. Their facial expressions betrayed no signs that they found his warbling unusual or inappropriate. The vast majority of them were from the Los Angeles area, so maybe, I mused, they found the "show biz" approach normal fare for a banquet talk. Again, after remarking how gloomy the outlook for our success, given the many legislative and court victories the pro-abortionists were winning throughout the country, he preached courage and determination, topping off his talk by singing two more verses, this time from "You'll Never Walk Alone." I suppose the evening was something like what was later to be known as "dinner theater."

I said above that we were graced at our conventions with some good speakers. An example is Mildred Jefferson. I had the pleasure of serving as a co-panelist with her at our statewide convention in the city of Oakland. She's every anti-abortionist's dream: black, female, non-Catholic, a member of the medical profession, and, to top matters off, highly intelligent and a sensational debater. Because she didn't match the stereotype of the anti-abortionist, it was harder for pro-abortionists to dodge the issue of killing the unborn by focusing on irrelevant factors like race, religion, or gender. The first black woman to go through Harvard's Medical School, she was known to return to Harvard, from time to time, to debate abortion with its feminist faculty members.

One year our statewide convention was held in San Francisco at the Fairmont Hotel. Again, a lot of people attended. I presented a paper on the right to life of deformed babies in which I challenged the view that the child's right to life depended on its being "wanted." Not surprisingly, pro-abortion protesters paraded back and forth in front of the hotel carrying placards about women's rights and reproductive freedom. Midway through my presentation, several of them entered the room. They stood in the back, wearing steely faces, as if waiting for me to say something that they could take back to headquarters as grist for their mill. I'm sure I disappointed them. I made no attacks on the pro-abortionists, attributed no skullduggery to them, but instead presented a cool, rational argument for the right of all innocent human beings, deformed or not, to life.

The banquet speaker was the late Morton Downey, Jr. All I knew about him at the time I'd learned from the "20/20" television program, which had devoted an unprecedented 60 minutes of one of its broadcasts

to coverage of the pro-life movement. The apparent reason for this generous allocation of programming was the movement's influence. Not only
had it succeeded in persuading voters to oust a couple of pro-abortion
legislators, it was, at that time, the show's narrator claimed, the most powerful Congressional lobbying group in America. The show featured
Downey as a major figure in the pro-life movement. In presenting him to
the audience, the mistress of ceremonies said that he'd won the Pulitzer
Prize for a volume of poetry, the title of which escapes me. At the banquet's
finish, I asked Downey for the book's publisher and he obliged me with it.
Unfortunately, that, too, has fled my memory. Since then I've heard no
mention of his name in connection with the Pulitzer Prize, but having
viewed his television show, I confess to having trouble imagining him as a
poet, let alone a prize winning one. He did, however, give an excellent
talk against euthanasia and what we nowadays call "physician-assisted suicide."

A DEMORALIZING BETRAYAL

The *Roe v. Wade* decision and the opportunism and lack of spine displayed
by our elected officials were not the only sources of our pessimism. The
defection of Jesse Jackson from the anti-abortion camp to the pro-choice
camp, a few years later, was crushing. I was a fan of his long before I found
out that he was against abortion. I admired his work on behalf of the
poor, the education of children, and his willingness to speak out against
the morally harmful influence of much of popular music and entertainment on our youth. So the discovery he was anti-abortion delighted me.

In the January 1977 edition of the *National Right to Life News,* he wrote
an article against abortion. Therein the Rev. Jackson met, head on, all the
major arguments for abortion: the fetus is not a human being, a woman
has the right to privacy, children with mental, physical, or socio-economic disadvantages are better off not being born, and so forth. What
perhaps made his argument so powerful was that he began it with the
revelation that he himself was illegitimate and that his mother had been
pressured to have an abortion. His concluding words are worth repeating:

What happens to the mind of a person, and the moral fabric of a nation, that accepts the aborting of the life of a baby without a pang of conscience? What kind of person, and what kind of society will we have in 20 years hence if life can be taken so casually?

It is that question, the question of our attitude, our value system, and our mind-set with regard to the nature and worth of life itself that is the central question confronting mankind. Failure to answer that question affirmatively may leave us with a hell right here on earth.

Such words give every indication of being firmly rooted in conviction. You can imagine the shock waves that rocked the anti-abortion ranks when, in 1983, Jackson "clarified" his stance on abortion by telling a group of feminist leaders that he favored keeping abortion legal. This revelation signaled his preparation for throwing his hat into the ring for the Democratic Party's presidential candidacy. The following year, 1984, the *Jesse Jackson for President Committee* issued a position paper on women's issues. About reproductive rights for women, it stated:

Even our Creator did not make us puppets, but gave us a free will to exercise a free choice. Thus, as a matter of public policy, I support the right of free choice relative to abortions. I am opposed to the Hyde Amendment because it denies equal protection under the law to all citizens. If abortions are legal for anyone, and they are, then they should be legal for everyone. Poor women should not be denied equal protection under the law because they are poor. I also oppose a Constitutional Amendment outlawing abortions. It is not right to impose private religious and moral positions on public policy as a matter of law, even though I support the right of all to differ and try to change public *attitudes* through personal persuasion. As a private matter, I would not, except in medically extenuating circumstances, advise a woman to have an abortion. I would also emphasize that while I fully support freedom of choice, that one must also be responsible and live with the consequences of one's choice. However, I repeat, I am strongly opposed to any legislation that would weaken or reverse the Supreme Court decision of *Roe v. Wade.*

It is one thing for a person whose position on abortion has all along been ambiguous or tentative to come out in favor of "choice" and "reproductive freedom." You can disagree with the decision without disrespecting the person. But it is quite another thing for someone who has emphatically condemned abortion as the destruction of innocent human life and who appeals to biology to support his claims about the human status of the unborn to make a complete turn-around. What new evidence came to light that led the Rev. Jackson to come out against the Hyde Amendment in 1984 when, in 1977, he'd sent the following "open letter" telegram to Congress?

> As a matter of conscience I must oppose the use of Federal funds for a policy of killing infants. The money would be much better expended to meet human needs. I am therefore urging that the Hyde Amendment be supported in the interest of a more humane policy and some new directions on issues for caring for the most precious resource we have – our children.

I lost all respect for the Reverend Jesse Jackson.

EXPOSING MY CHILDREN TO THE BATTLE

Even when my children were very young, as early as seven and eight years old, I would bring them with me to my debates whenever I could. I wanted them to know what I was doing and why it was important to do it. When my son, Mark, was seven years old, I brought him with me to a lecture I gave in Santa Clara to a pro-life group. In the course of explaining why an indirect abortion, as when a pregnant woman has a cancerous uterus, can be morally justified, I gave the following example. A man operates a drawbridge for a living. Every day at 4pm he must raise the bridge to allow the entry of cargo ships into the harbor; at 5pm he must lower the bridge again for the commuter train, carrying hundreds of passengers, to cross it. One particular day, the man brings his very young son to work with him. From all appearances, it's easy babysitting job because the child is protected and easily supervised in the small cabin where his father operates the drawbridge. At 4pm he raises the bridge to let the ships through. When it's time to lower the bridge, he notices, to his horror, that his son has managed to climb in among the gears that raise and lower the bridge. There isn't time to get him out since the train will soon be at the bridge. If he fails to lower the bridge, hundreds of passengers will be killed and injured; but if he lowers the bridge, his son will be crushed to death by the meshing gears. He lowers the bridge. I explained to my audience that the bridge operator did the right thing and that the killing of his son was morally justified as an *indirect* killing. It's called "indirect" because killing the child was not a necessary condition for lowering the bridge; his presence among the gears was accidental to the necessity of meshing the gears to lower the bridge.

When we got home, Mark announced to his mother, "Mommie, Daddy said he would kill me." Until then I didn't realize how much children personalize what they see and hear.

That realization led me to wonder how forceful was the impression made on our youngest child, Rosalind, when she ran into my study one day without warning while I was inspecting an array of 5 x 7 color photographs of aborted children spread over my desk. I immediately shoved them into a pile and covered them with my briefcase. She said nothing about the pictures, so I said nothing about them. She was four years old then. Some months later when my older children and I were discussing abortion, Rosalind said matter-of-factly,

"Chopped up babies."

CLASSROOM LECTURES AND "ONE NIGHT STANDS"

During my thirty-six years teaching philosophy, I've taught some form of ethics course – general ethics, bioethics, and social ethics – almost every semester. I've thus had the opportunity to give thorough, systematic lectures on and against induced abortion. I get to discourse on the foundations of ethics, ethical theories, to defend a natural law ethics over utilitarian, deontological, and relativist ethics, and cover the history of abortion in the West, the ontology of human nature and personhood, the meaning of "human rights," the evidence from embryology and fetology – in short, to discourse on all the things that are presupposed for a rational and constructive assessment of the arguments for and against abortion.

Debates and public lectures don't allow anything close to a thorough approach to abortion or to any other topic. Crucial presuppositions, such as those listed above, must be ignored. Nevertheless these "one night stands" offer precious opportunities to address people who otherwise would never hear a rational argument against induced abortion. The challenge is to get your message across in a very short span of time. This means that your argument must have a lean, sharp cutting edge and that you must go for sudden impact. After many years and many mistakes, I think I've attained a reasonable degree of effectiveness in those things. Chapters 5 and 6 of this book contain what I've learned about debating abortion and what kind of arguments I present in debates and public lectures on the subject.

Besides speaking on abortion in my classes, I frequently debate the issue at the University of California, at Berkeley, Stanford University, local law schools, high schools as well as on radio and television. I intend to continue this activity until I check out or become so "lost in senile rapture," to borrow from Mark Twain, that I can no longer give effective witness to the truth. What distresses me is the lack of successors to this work. I'm only speaking about what I see, or don't see, in my own area; hopefully, other areas of the country have more young men and women entering the pro-life ranks. As I say in Chapter 5, I think that young women are the most effective anti-abortion speakers because women in the audience can identify with them.

BRIGHTER PROSPECTS

My overall assessment of the abortion debate in America is that anti-abortionists are winning, slowly but surely. You can see this in the surveys that repeatedly show that the American public is increasingly uneasy about the matter, particularly about abortion on request. Abortion is the bone in the throat of contemporary American society that slavery was in 19th century. Consider, for example, the 1993 decision of the California State Supreme Court, California's *People v. Davis*, that a third party who kills a fetus can be tried for murder even if the fetus is pre-viable. The court hastened to add that this ruling did not overturn a woman's Constitutional right to an abortion. This judicial balancing act recalls the line in Dickens' *Oliver Twist*: "If the law says that, sir, then the law is an ass." Just as it must have stretched credulity to convince oneself that African Americans were intrinsically inferior as human beings and thus could justifiably be treated as personal property, so the idea of the fetus as somehow sub-human, although still a member of the human species, must seem to us, in our honest moments, as preposterous. A human father and a human mother produce the human fetus; if it's not a human being, what is it? Why is its destruction by a third party called "murder" while its destruction by the woman carrying it is called an exercise in the Constitutionally protected right to privacy? After all, it's the same being that is destroyed. Since when does murder depend on which private party does the killing?

I suspect that the public witness against abortion, most of it given by ordinary folks, many of whom are housewives and mothers, has largely contributed to the uneasiness of the American conscience. No matter how formidable the odds against changing the abortion mentality, public witness remains powerful. As I observed in Chapter 1, the intellect turns to the truth just as spontaneously as the eye turns to the light and the ear to sound.

CHAPTER THREE

THE MAN WHO WOULDN'T HAVE AN ABORTION

"And now, in this despicable age, no maiden can be safe even if one were to hide and enclose her in another labyrinth like the Minotaur's; because here too, through crevices in the rock or in the very air, the pestilence of love will reach her with zealous and damnable insistence, and despite all islolation she will come to ruin. And so, as age succeeded age and wickedness increased, the Order of Knights Errant was instituted for the general safety of all, to defend maidens, protect widows and come to the aid of orphans and paupers."

The Adventures of Don Quixote, Pt I, Ch XI

AN UNLIKELY CANDIDATE FOR ABORTION

A couple of years ago, I taught a course on the social teachings of the Church for the Pastoral Leadership Program in the San Francisco Catholic Archdiocese. One evening, after having lectured on abortion, one of the students caught up with me as I was leaving the school building for the parking lot. My guess is that he was somewhere in his mid to late forties. With his bushy, mussed hair, baggy pants, belly sagging over his belt, and shirt sloppily tucked around his belt line, he always presented a disheveled appearance. If you spotted him heading toward your desk for a job interview, you'd decide not to give him the job even before he opened his mouth. He'd approached me several times in the semester, during class breaks, and always uttered the same complaint about landlords in the city evicting tenants just to raise rents or refurbish. He apparently thought it a fit topic for discussion since the course was about the Catholic Church's view of justice; besides, he was one of the unlucky tenants.

But on this particular occasion, he had something different to say. As a young man, his live-in girlfriend got pregnant by him and went through with an abortion despite all his pleas and protests. That ended the relationship. He later married and when the marriage was ending in divorce, his pregnant wife announced her plans to have an abortion. But this time, his pleading succeeded. Promising to raise the child himself, she gave him unfettered custody of the child when it was born. Good to his promise, he did raise the child all by himself and would, in a few days from now, have the joy of being present at his son's graduation from the university.

All of which leads me to proclaim to Sally Markowitz and Andrea Dworkin and all the other "victim feminists" in the world: "What a relief it is to know that all men are not pigs!"

But enough about men. If any group has a reason for ducking the question, "Does abortion kill an innocent human being?," it's the women who've had abortions. But my acquaintance with a few of them reveals that, as much as they may try to keep from thinking about what they've done, they live every day in the knowledge that they've killed their unborn baby.

WAS I CHAFFEUR FOR THE EXECUTION OF AN UNBORN CHILD?

She was in her senior year at the University of San Francisco when I first met her. We used to talk frequently. Although never my student, our paths crossed regularly. She came to the U.S. when she was eighteen years old to attend the university. She had an American boyfriend on whom she apparently doted: she would clean his apartment weekly; on Sundays after church she would bring coffee and pastry to his bedside – no early riser he! It seems he had deflowered her and there was some promise of marriage down the road. She didn't work too hard at concealing the fact that he treated her shabbily. Besides exploiting her for housekeeping and room service (appealing to her nurturing and nesting instincts), he was also unfaithful to her. Occasionally while cleaning his apartment, she would find other women's apparel under the bed.

Upon graduation she secured a job on the east coast. One evening several months later, I got a call from her. She told me tearfully that she was pregnant. A Brazilian, whom she was dating, was the father. She was "on the pill," but decided to go off it even though they continued to be intimate. She never explained her decision. Shortly after, she got pregnant. He offered to marry her, but she declined. I countered her talk of abortion by promising to put her in touch with the Birthright agency in her locale as well as with a priest I knew in D.C. who was orthodox, practical and sensitive. I explained that Birthright existed to encourage single women to carry their pregnancies to term and to provide them with support, medical, psychological, financial and so forth. She wanted the abortion because she couldn't bear to have her coworkers gossiping about her and laughing behind her back. Worst of all, she protested, was having to face her parents. The next day I called her back with the promised information.

My encouragement didn't work. Several weeks later she came to San Francisco to stay with her brother for the Christmas holidays. We went to lunch and I knew something was wrong because she seemed defensive throughout. She'd seen the priest to whom I referred her, but apparently made no effort to get in touch with Birthright. After lunch, she told me she had an appointment to see her physician at a hospital in the city and accepted my offer to drive her there. A couple of days later, I understood why she was defensive. She called me at home in the evening to inform me, between sobs, that she'd got the abortion. Apparently, she'd made up her mind to go ahead with it before she called me for lunch. That means I've got to face the possibility that I unwittingly volunteered to serve as the chauffeur for the assassination of her unborn child. Hopefully that was not the day of the abortion but only the first meeting with the physician who would perform it. One of life's many ironies: I was almost stillborn; I was a breach birth and entered the world with the umbilical cord wrapped tightly about my neck. The physician couldn't get me to cry and was about to tell my mother that I didn't make it when the senior physician on duty came by and decided to give me one more slap on the butt. I started crying. There's the irony. Every day countless newborn babies are saved in hospitals and yet countless unborn babies are killed in those same hospitals.

She phoned me several days after she'd returned to the east coast. She told me, once again through her sobbing, that she'd had the abortion and how terrible she felt. What brought on the episode of remorse was a demonstration outside her place of work by a feminist group who were chanting for abortion rights and reproductive freedom. She told me how womanly she felt when she was pregnant: "Professor Dennehy, my breasts were getting bigger and I felt life inside me. Now they're getting smaller and when I go to the toilet, I see blood."

Her remorse didn't last forever. The following year she phoned me to say she was in San Francisco to attend a wedding. She'd seen me on television that morning and decided to see if we could have lunch. During the meal she volunteered that she'd had another abortion. It seems she was then having affairs with three men. "How are your dreams?" I asked. "Terrible," she answered. I didn't press for details. It was clear that, her earlier remorse notwithstanding, abortion had become her quick fix.

"OUT, OUT, DAMNED SPOT"

Another student of mine revealed to me that she'd had three abortions. I suspect that the revelation was made out of self-defense. She knew that I debated abortion in public (she may have seen me on local television, debating one of the city supervisors or Planned Parenthood representatives) and my presence before her in the classroom probably floated her deep-seated guilt to the surface. Her first abortion was performed back in her Asian hometown when she was seventeen and a senior in high school. She insisted that the procedure was necessary because being pregnant out of wedlock would have made her situation intolerable in that culture. Several years later, her fiancé impregnated her, but she broke off the engagement upon learning of his infidelity, and that led to her second abortion. When she came to the United States, she eventually got an American live-in boyfriend. After two years in that arrangement, she ended the relationship, but not before realizing she was pregnant. That explains abortion number three.

About a year later, we had occasion to meet again. In the course of our conversation, she mentioned that she'd recently had a terrible dream. She dreamed she'd returned to her homeland to visit her family. She entered her parents' home only to find no one there. The walls of the rooms were splattered with blood.

My interpretation then, as now, was Freudian. I know, Freud's no longer in fashion, but, in this case, the plausibility of a Freudian interpretation is compelling: The rooms in her parents' home were really dream-symbols for her womb. It wasn't the house that was empty but her own womb. The blood-splattered walls symbolized the blood from her unborn children. And her surprise at finding no family member at home when they were expecting her, when they should have been there to welcome her upon her arrival, symbolized her deep sense of loss and disappointment for the absence of the three children she should have welcomed into the world since she was carrying them within herself. I didn't impart my interpretation of the dream to her.

THE REPLACEMENT PREGNANCY

A former student exemplified a more complex abortion motivation. She was smart and her writing showed literary talent. She came by my office one afternoon ostensibly to talk about the course. But it only took a few minutes of conversation to see that she'd come to talk about her life and future prospects. She revealed that she'd had an abortion in her senior year of high school, but subsequently came to regret it; having reached the conclusion that induced abortion is morally unjustifiable. She described how it all happened. In the evenings, she and her boyfriend would frequently drive to a lake on the outskirts of her hometown where they would smoke cigarettes and drink beer. That's where she got pregnant. She said that he offered to marry her, but she declined because his prospects as a provider were not promising. He was then doing menial work in a pizza parlor and, so far as she could tell, showed no desire to leave that job or to earn more money. She indicated that her decision to get an abortion was also tied to concerns over the health of the child. Her boyfriend regularly smoked marijuana and she'd heard about the studies that showed a correlation between the use of that drug and chromosomal damage to offspring.

Financial problems kept her out of school the following semester. Instead she got a job in her hometown as a waitress. Months later, I learned from a student who was a close friend of hers that she was pregnant again and that the father was her old boyfriend. This struck me at the time as a classic example of what psychiatrists call the "replacement baby syndrome." The expression refers to a woman who gets pregnant a year or two after her abortion, hoping to replace the baby she aborted. In my student's case, she not only got pregnant again in a relatively short time after her abortion, but by the same man, the one she feared was incapable of siring genetically healthy children and being a decent provider!

A couple of years later, she had another child out of wedlock, this time by a different man. About ten years have now past since the birth of the second child and she remains unmarried. I understand that she has psychological problems and is on medication. Maybe these problems contributed to her less than rational behavior from the start.

AN UNREPENTANT SOUL IN DISTRESS

The thinking of some women who admit to having had an abortion has always mystified me. I remember one in particular. I'd just finished speaking on abortion to a class at Canãda Community College, located a short drive south of San Francisco. A woman in her early thirties approached me after everyone else had left the room. Her looks were striking. She was tall and statuesque, with luxurious, cascading red hair and large brown eyes. After introducing herself she expressed her agreement with everything I'd said in my presentation. She told me that she was recently divorced and had two teenage sons. Then she revealed that she'd had an abortion because she couldn't tell whether her estranged husband or her current boyfriend caused her pregnancy. She told me that before then she'd been active in pro-life groups, doing things like manning telephone hotlines for pregnant women. She made it plain that she had no doubts that the fetus was a human being.

More recently still, she'd had herself sterilized. She thought it odd that it was so easy to get an abortion but difficult to get sterilized. For the latter, she had to undergo a session with a psychiatrist and get his written recommendation that she be permitted to have her tubes tied. I suggested that that was because sterilization is permanent and she might change her mind and want another child. She told me of the psychiatrist's warning: "You may fall in love with someone and want to have his child; but if you're sterilized you won't be able to." She replied, "Doctor, that's exactly why I want to be sterilized." She got the sterilization.

Two things struck me about this meeting and, indeed, have stayed with me over the years. The first was that, even though she knew that the fetus was a human being, she seemed completely unrepentant about the abortion. The second was her manner. She wasn't defensive, hostile or aggressive during our conversation but was instead disarmingly feminine and gentle. But she couldn't conceal – maybe she didn't care to – a melancholy and resignation. It was all so sad, as if she knew beforehand that it was wrong, but had convinced herself to do it anyway and live with it. I could only think that somewhere in her marriage she'd been so hurt that..... Well, who knows?

PSYCHOLOGICAL HARM

Then there was the woman at a local state college. I'd given a public lecture against abortion and was replying to questions and comments from the audience. One woman stood up and said that she could testify to the psychological harm that abortion does to the women who have them. She confessed to having had an abortion a few years back and claimed to have suffered emotionally ever since. Her way of talking and her general manner strongly suggested that she was unstable. But no sooner had she finished speaking than another woman stood up to announce that she'd had seven abortions and she felt fine. This incident is an example of why I never base my arguments against abortion on bad medical, psychological or social consequences, even if I have supporting empirical and statistical evidence. It's an approach that invites the interpretation that if it weren't for the bad consequences, abortion would be justifiable. Besides, I can't recall any debate, regardless of the issue, in which the citation of data to support the claim of bad consequences, by one of the participants, was not countered by citation of statistical findings to the contrary. And since it's a safe bet that hardly anyone in the audience will take the trouble to check the conflicting statistical claims, the general impression is that your argument has been nullified.

DOES SHE KNOW SHE'S KILLING A HUMAN BEING?

My impression is that women who get abortions know in their heart of hearts that what's inside them is a human being. For example, one student told me that when she found she was pregnant, she gave up eating junk food in favor of fruits and vegetables, etc. She said, "I was determined that that baby was going to be well nourished as long as I carried it." Another remorsefully said, "My baby would have been a year old tomorrow." I'll never forget one scene that occurred a few years before abortion had become a public issue. I was at the home of a fellow graduate student in Berkeley. After dinner, his wife, who was an artist, brought their infant son from the bedroom. What stays in my mind is the absolute incongruity between the maternal pose of her holding the child in her arms while at the same time recounting how she'd unsuccessfully tried to have it legally aborted.

A BATTERED WIFE

Another woman told me the following story. She'd been in an unhappy marriage. Her husband used cocaine and was given to violent outbursts of temper that frequently led to physically abusing her. One day while they were driving down the road, she told him she was pregnant. He abruptly turned the car off the road as if to drive it into the lake. After regaining his composure, he said to her, "If you want to stay married, you'd better get an abortion." She was at the time psychologically weak and feared abandonment. She got the abortion to keep him from leaving her.

Her reflections on the abortion itself, I suspect, are common (universal?) with women who undergo the procedure. The doctor who performed the abortion had been her physician for some time. He had always been warm and friendly. But during the operation itself, his attitude changed; he seemed angry and harsh. He used cold water – "splashed it," I think she said – on her vagina and his actions were rough, as if making no effort to be gentle. She, meanwhile, entertained the hope that he wouldn't go through with it; she wanted to scream, "Stop!" but couldn't seem to speak. When she finally said she'd changed her mind, that she didn't want the abortion, it was too late. She admitted to knowing all along that she was killing her child.

Why the change of attitude in her physician? Was he trying to discourage her from having subsequent abortions by making it an unpleasant experience? A Baptist, maybe he was really displacing his anger with himself for doing something he believed to be wrong.

Her husband picked her up at the clinic. As they were driving home, she told him she was hungry and asked if they could pull into a fast food restaurant for a burger. He refused, saying he was in a hurry to get home so he could catch a basketball game on television. What a guy!

This woman insisted that all women who get abortions know that they've killed their unborn child. Myself, I've always wondered if that isn't the reason women who defend abortion so frequently get angry and strident, sometimes trying to break up the discussion or disrupt the class by protesting the time spent on that subject or walking out of the classroom: deep down they know what they've done, but won't admit it to themselves. This particular woman told me that getting the abortion was the worst thing she's ever done. She's a Catholic and has been given absolution for her sin, but complains that she's not yet been able to forgive herself. I'm convinced that it's just because women who defend abortion know that abortion does kill innocent human beings that my opponents in debate avoid the question, "Is the fetus a human being," like the plague.

This same woman offers an observation about the effect of legalization on the national abortion rate. She insists that if abortion had been illegal, she'd never have procured one. I think this is generally true, despite the persistent claim from abortion advocates that, legal or not, women will continue to have abortions. But where is the evidence for this? Any figures given for the number of illegal abortions should be viewed skeptically for the simple reason that back alley abortionists are not in the habit of keeping written records. Formerly a leading abortion advocate and now a leading anti-abortionist, Dr. Bernard Nathanson possesses impeccable credentials when it comes to commenting on abortion figures. Not only did he preside over a New York City abortion clinic that performed 75,000 abortions, he was also one of the founders of National Association for the Repeal of Abortion Laws (NARAL). He writes that, in order to create public sympathy for permissive abortion laws, he and his colleagues lied about the number of illegal abortions performed annually in the United States: "The actual figure was approaching 100,000 but the figure we gave to the media repeatedly was 1,000,000...The number of women dying from illegal abortions was around 200-250 annually. The figure we constantly fed to the media was 10,000."

Once society legalizes a practice, it becomes conventionally acceptable and then morally acceptable. The legalization of induced abortion has created an abortion mentality. Combined with pro-abortion propaganda, complicity by the media and so-called social leaders, like politicians, clergy, judges, physicians, attorneys and teachers, the legalization of abortion allows women and their male partners to play games with themselves: "It must be all right to get one because the Supreme Court of the United States says it's a woman's right; women have to protect their reproductive freedom; it's the intelligent thing to do, etc."

But self-deception is a game that never works; it's like cheating at solitaire; who is being fooled? Women know that when pregnant, they're carrying a human being inside them and if they abort it, they know that they've done more than "terminate the pregnancy"; they know that they've killed their unborn child.

ABORTION IS BIRTH CONTROL AFTER THE FACT

Who gets abortions? The vast majority of the women I knew who got abortions did it for birth control; you might say it's birth control after the fact. In a culture that blinks at promiscuity, widespread abortion is inevitable. I can't say how greatly the advent of "the pill" contributed to the sexual revolution that started in the 1960s, but I suspect its effect was cataclysmic. Until then premarital sex was nowhere near so common as today because, as Graham Greene has one of his characters say, "Nothing dampens romance like the thought of babies." With the fear of pregnancy out of the way, the sexual revolution seemed practical.

Some people scoff at the idea that premarital sex is more common today than before, but either they are simply in denial or they weren't around to acquire a before-the-pill/after-the-pill perspective. An accurate way of settling the question is to check the sexually transmitted disease rate in the nation before the advent of the pill and compare it with the rate afterwards. Since the pill came on the scene, the rate of sexually transmitted diseases has soared. This is a reliable sign of sexual promiscuity since these diseases are associated with multiple sexual partners. The fact that the pill was not a prophylactic proved no deterrent to the newly found "sexual freedom" because the traditional sexually transmitted diseases, like syphilis and gonorrhea, were easily cured with a shot of penicillin.

What took some of the wind out of the sails of the sexual revolution was the emergence of genital herpes and AIDS. Although controllable, herpes remains in the subject for life, breaking out, from time to time, in what can be painful, and sometimes fatal, episodes; and AIDS is both incurable and fatal. Nevertheless, the sexual revolution had changed the sexual behavior of our culture and fear of disease not withstanding, the pill remained the preferred method of contraception. When columnist Lucius Beebe wrote years ago that "contraceptives are distressing and untidy," he had in mind condoms, diaphragms, gels and foams. He was right. Men don't like to suit up for sex and the consensus seems to be that the spontaneity and "magic" of sexual intercourse evaporate if the woman has to interrupt foreplay to insert various devices. So before the heterosexual community began to fear they, too, could contract AIDS, the pill reigned supreme.

But the problem with any contraceptive is the problem with any human device: it has to be used, and used properly. And thereby hangs a tale. The decision to use contraceptives must negotiate with the subjective factor. Some women stop taking the pill because they've heard that it can lead to strokes; others stop because it makes them puffy. Most interesting is that some women entertain the fantasy of being swept off their feet, of being "taken" or ravished by the man. Taking the pill collides with that fantasy because it implies premeditation to have sex. Whatever the reason, the fact is that a large number of women who get pregnant out of wedlock know about contraceptives and have access to them, but decide not to use them. If a woman gets pregnant and doesn't want to be, there's always the safety net of abortion. "You have a right to have sex and abortion is your quick fix if you need it." That's the deceptive message offered to our young people today.

CHAPTER FOUR

BAD COMPANIONS

"I have to tell you, my lord, that if your lordship doesn't settle down and stay quitely at home, and leave off going up mountains and down valleys like a tormented soul, searching for so-called adventures that I prefer to call misfortunes, I'll have to raise my voice and complain loudly to both God and king to put an end to it "

The Adventures of Don Quixote Part II, Ch. VI

The pro-abortionists have been successful in deflecting public attention from the unspeakable act of deliberately killing unborn babies to the violence perpetrated against abortion doctors and their staff. I don't recall ever having met anyone in the anti-abortion movement who advocated violence, or even seemed the type to do mayhem against abortionists or their facilities. But every movement has its share of boors and jerks, and I've met my share of them.

THE INTIMIDATOR

There was one guy, tall and physically imposing, with an intimidating manner. With a big-boned body accentuating his small head, he always reminded me of "Brutus," the goonish character in the *Popeye* comic strip

For a short while he was with our United For Life group in Santa Clara. This was a time when members of our group were frequently invited to speak in public schools in the area and he was one of our speakers. One day he told several of us over coffee how he and one of the administrators at the high school where he had just finished speaking happened to cross paths in the school parking lot. The administrator criticized his anti–abortion position. He briefly described their disagreement, and then bragged about leaving the administrator lying on the ground, "gurgling in his own blood." The quoted words are verbatim. Even though almost forty years have passed since that conversation, I recall his words vividly not only because he took such relish in uttering them but also because of his presumption in supposing that our response would be one of admiration or approval rather than shock and disgust. I suspect that the episode was all in his mind and never really happened. At all events, one thing was clear: he liked physical intimidation and wallowed in the *persona* of the violent man.

Another member of our group related to me a second episode involving him. In the early days of the anti–abortion movement, I'm thinking of 1968-70 or so, we were big on showing slides of fetal development and aborted fetuses in our presentations. In our naiveté we thought that when people saw such graphic evidence of what abortion was and what it did, they wouldn't support the pro–abortion position. In our dreams! Apparently, while he was showing the slides to a junior high school class one day, he became increasingly angry at the showing of each successive slide until he finally began shoving the slide feeder into the projector with such force that he broke it.

As mentioned above, he was only with our group for a short while. We soon lost contact with him for good, and I can't recall anyone in United For Life expressing sorrow over it. The irony in the whole thing was that he was a salesman for air-conditioning units. Either he was a Dr. J ekyll/Mr. Hyde personality or he was a larger–than–life testimonial to the merits of the best-selling book of a few years back, *Selling by Intimidation*. About a year later, I heard that he and his wife had separated. Apparently, she wasn't such an easy sell. Aside from him, I never met anyone in the pro-life movement who struck me as inclined to violence, let alone any-one who was likely to engage in mayhem against pro-abortionists.

CRAZY AND STRONG DON'T MIX

There was another occasion when I witnessed behavior by someone on the pro-life side that could hardly be regarded as flattering to our cause. But he was obviously a trifle unhinged mentally and didn't look like someone capable of engaging in violence with malice aforethought. The year was 1967. I've already recounted how a few busloads of us from the San Francisco Bay Area and the South Bay went to Sacramento for the Senate Judiciary Committee's public hearing on Beilenson's proposed "Therapeutic Abortion Act." It was bad enough that we had to wait for several hours in a hallway before being admitted to the hearing room; but waiting alongside us were the pro-abortion contingent. I tried to strike up a conversation with a rather attractive young woman from their ranks who was standing right across from me. I don't recall what I said, aside from its being mere chit-chat, but I must have mentioned my wife; for I do remember her reply: "I'm surprised any woman would marry you."

Our unhinged colleague was in his late twenties or early thirties and claimed to be a law student in Sacramento. The incident in question oc-curred when he got into a disagreement with one of the pro-abortion women over who ought to be in front of whom in the line. He stepped in front of her; she pushed against him with her arms; without turning to face her he elbowed her several times in the chest and in retaliation she punched him in the back. My friend, Frank Filice, persuaded him to calm down and the matter ended there. I wasn't the only one breathing a sigh of relief. The guy was about six feet six with broad shoulders and large forearms. Things might have gotten ugly. During the hearing, he inter-rupted Senator Belienson's presentation a couple of times by exclaiming, "Fallacy! Fallacy!" but remained silent for the rest of the session after an equally imposing sergeant-at-arms informed him that if there were any-more outbursts he would be escorted out of the room.

WITH BOORISH PARTNERS, DO WE NEED OPPONENTS?

If not violent pro-lifers, what about boorish ones? Boorishness is not violence, but boorish people hurt our movement nonetheless. So, instead of "bad companions," I'll call them "annoying companions."

Recently, I had a debate partner, an attorney, over at the University of California, Berkeley, whose brand of boorishness really hurts the cause. Aggressive and pushy, he alienated the large audience of students by talking about what he wanted to talk about instead of answering their questions. He also had trouble shutting up. Even though there were four of us on stage, two speakers on each side, he commandeered almost all the time available for responding to the audience's questions and comments. I'm sure the audience left the auditorium with the impression that he was either insecure or simply out to "win" the debate.

WHAT DOES VIOLENCE HAVE TO DO WITH THE CAUSE?

The outbreaks of violence against abortion clinics and the physicians who perform abortions provide grist for the mills of the pro-abortionists. They don't hesitate to point to these incidents as dramatic revelations of the true enemies of life: the anti-choice people. You can't deny that there is, at least, the appearance of hypocrisy and deceit in the conduct of those in the pro-life ranks who, under the banner of defending human life, would justify the killing of human beings. A Freudian explanation of their behavior might be seen as a classic case of the *Id* outwitting the *Superego*. The aggressive instincts of the *Id* move the anti-abortionist to do violence to the abortionist, but the Superego intervenes with its moral sensibilities, moving the subject to curb his desires for aggression. If, however, the subject thinks that doing violence to the abortionist is necessary to stop the wholesale slaughter of the unborn and to preserve democratic society, then it is morally justifiable because the attack is now seen as part of a holy war. Thus both *Superego* and *Id* are satisfied.

I don't doubt that some mechanism like that propels many fanatics to do violence. It would be surprising if that mechanism were not operative in the decision of sadists to enter law enforcement and military service. Punitive attacks in wartime, such as the allied firebombing of Dresden, are a good example. And while the decision to drop nuclear bombs on the Japanese cities of Hiroshima and Nagasaki was not punitive in intent but defensive (President Harry Truman believed that the alternative, a landing assault on the main Japanese island, Honshu, would result in 900,000 U.S. casualties), it is not in the least implausible that many Americans, civilian as well as military, were able to indulge their aggressive instincts toward the Japanese for starting the war by seeing those two cities pulverized, despite the fact that the bombing killed or injured hundreds of thousands of Japanese civilians.

No movement that has to struggle against laws and other forms of institutional resistance to attain what it regards as justice can insulate itself from the infiltration of at least some fanatical and violent people. Social protest movements are magnets for violent personalities. Those who condemn the pro-life movement for the violence against abortionists and their clinics seem to forget that the violence is perpetrated by what is at most a mere handful of anti-abortion sympathizers. They also seem conveniently to ignore the violent tactics adopted at the start of the 20th century in England by some suffragettes: such as the militant Women's Suffrage and Political Union, founded by Emmeline Pankhurst in 1903, which employed bombing in addition to the tactics of boycotting and picketing; and also seem to ignore the tactics of armed assault used by the abolitionists in the United States in the 19th century, and by some Civil Rights sympathizers in the 1960s. Even though the Civil Rights protest started in North Carolina as a non-violent movement, some of the protesters grew impatient with the progress of the movement and began to burn cities.

My point is that Woman Suffrage, the abolition of slavery, the Civil Rights movement and the pro-life effort must be evaluated on their own merits. Who would say, for example, that the John Brown episode invalidated the legitimacy of the anti-slavery movement? If the pro-life movement lacks moral legitimacy, it cannot be because of the immoral behavior of a few violent people. It could only be so because the following were true: the human fetus is not a human being; a woman has the moral right to decide whether her unborn child shall continue to live; society can protect its future if it exercises the right to decide which of the unborn shall be allowed to see the light of day.

That said, there can be no justification for violence against abortionists and their facilities, and those who engage in it ought to be punished. Society cannot tolerate vigilantism. The state of Florida did the right thing by imposing a life sentence on the man who shot down an abortionist and his bodyguard in cold blood outside a Tallahassee abortion clinic. Yet the killing that goes on inside the abortion clinic (better named "abortion chamber") is more heinous than the killing of the abortionist. The slaughtered unborn, after all, have harmed no one, have committed no crime and endanger the life and well being of no one. Meanwhile, the abortionist doesn't even know his victims: he engages in the wholesale killing of anonymous, innocent human beings for profit.

An interesting case was related to me by a New Jersey attorney, whom I met at the National Conference on Abortion and Public Policy that convened at St. Louis University in March, 1993. He was about sixty years old and had, by then, confined his practice to defending pro-life cases. It seems his client had entered a clinic, where his estranged wife was about to have an abortion, and held the abortionist prisoner in one of the rooms. The husband was arrested and charged. The attorney told me that he sought to defend him by appealing to any father's natural instinct to defend the life of his child in the face of imminent death, but the judge would not even allow that defense to be heard in court.

Cases of this kind belong to a category quite separate from acts of violence done against abortionists and their facilities in the name of the abstract principle of protecting the unborn. Consider: first, the man believes that his unborn child is a human being; second, he disagrees with the woman's resolution to abort the child; third, he has exhausted all nonviolent means of preventing the abortion, persuasion, court intervention, etc. Is it not reasonable, perhaps a matter of moral obligation, to boot, for him to employ force to try to prevent the killing of his child? Here we have a powerful example of the primal violence against nature which abortion constitutes.

Because the practice of elective abortion has been institutionalized, it has also been "morally" sanitized. A third party who tries to halt an abortion is regarded as criminally violent because he seeks to interfere with a

Constitutionally protected act. But the violence that the abortionist inflicts on the unborn at the woman's request, even though unmistakable, is veiled under euphemisms such as the "termination of pregnancy," while the victim is removed from the human race by the numbing term, "fetus." In the previous chapter, I said that, in my thirty-six years of debating abortion, hardly any of my opponents (I can recall no more than two) were willing to address, in any serious way, the fundamental question, Is the unborn baby a human being? It seems reasonable to me that anyone genuinely concerned about human life and dignity would address that question immediately. The stubborn refusal of pro-abortionists to open the question for public discussion, given the overwhelming evidence for the humanity of the unborn, leads me to suspect that they know what the procedure is about, but either cannot face what they themselves have done or see abortion as instrumental to some higher commitment that they do not wish to jeopardize by inquiring into "secondary" discussions about the unborn's status.

At all events, elective abortion constitutes such primal violence, especially when performed in wholesale fashion, that I, for one, don't see what can stop its murderous ethos from spilling over the walls of the abortion clinics and flooding society at large. You can see that this has already begun from the current movement in favor of physician-assisted suicide and the movement's consequent winking at involuntary euthanasia, to wit, the policy of refusing to treat severely afflicted newborns suffering from Down's syndrome and spina bifida, even though those conditions are independent of the afflictions for which treatment is denied. Helga Kuhse and Peter Singer could not have put matters more bluntly in the preface to their book, *Should the Baby Live?*: "We think that some severely afflicted infants should be killed." Notice that they do not say "allowed to die" but "killed." Several years ago, shortly after the unfrocked Episcopal clergyman in Tallahassee had fatally shot the abortionist, I remember an intriguing observation offered by philosophy professor Russell Hittinger. Although quick to admit that the shooting was unjustifiable, Hittinger went on to say that it was almost predictable; for once society relinquishes to women its exclusive possession of the franchise to use violence so they can have abortions, it becomes difficult to keep other members of society from believing that they, too, have a right to that franchise.

The legitimacy of state authority over its members rests on justice. The goal of political society is the promotion and protection of the common good, and the state, which is the uppermost agency of political society, is authorized to use power, if needed, for those ends. When the state uses power unjustly, it undermines its own legitimacy and can no longer claim exclusive franchises, such as the death penalty. Consider, again, the decision rendered by the California State Supreme Court in *People v. Davis*. The court ruled that a third party who kills a fetus, even though nonviable, can be charged with murder, but a woman who kills her own fetus in a legal abortion is simply exercising her Constitutional right to privacy. Because an innocent human being is killed in both cases, the attempt to criminalize the one and not the other degrades the category of murder into the most transparent of legal fictions.

If it is practically impossible to exclude violent people from the ranks of organizations committed to social reforms, how can the pro-life movement be expected to keep at bay sympathizers who think violence against abortionists is morally justifiable? No doubt, some of these fringe members see themselves as freedom fighters protecting the lives of the unborn against assault by a morally corrupt regime; others perhaps see themselves as participants in a Hobbesian state of nature where "war of all against all" and "kill or be killed" are the rules of survival.

One of my colleagues, a Ph.D. in biology who possesses the kind of lucid intellect that catches your immediate attention, once asked me why attacks on abortion clinics would not be morally justified for the same reason that Thomas Aquinas justified the killing of an unjust king. The difference between the two kinds of acts, however, is that legalized abortion in a democratic society does not match the conditions that Aquinas advances for justifiable regicide. For one thing, he says that all other means of deposing the unjust ruler must be tried. We have means other than violence for ending legal abortion; for example, electing pro-life lawmakers, which we are doing, and passing pro-life legislation through Congress, which we are also doing. Indeed, my own perception is that slowly but surely the public is getting the pro-life message and displaying increasing reservations about elective abortions.

Another condition Aquinas stipulates is that there must be good reasons for believing that the regicide will not produce worse injustice in society than presently exists. Violence against abortionists might succeed in closing down their clinics and discouraging physicians from doing abortions. To some extent, this may already have happened. But even so, it seems likely that the social evils would increase. After all, is it reasonable to suppose that the justification for vigilantism can be confined to the eradication of abortion facilities and the people who use them? On the contrary, what we could expect is social anarchy with various citizens' groups taking arms against social practices, which they deemed heinous but against which nonviolent means of reform have proved ineffective. We are already witnessing groups that use bombs and flames to destroy facilities that they believe are harming animals and wilderness areas.

LET'S TALK ABOUT *ALL* THE VIOLENCE

Violence in society is, however, a two-edged sword. If you think that citizen violence against abortionists could unleash violent attacks against other perceived social evils, will you entertain the possibility that the institutionalized practice of abortion could unleash other forms of violence? Let me repeat what I said above: I cannot help wondering if the increasing violence in our society is not related to the legalized, wholesale killing of the unborn. Everybody agrees that the bombing of the Federal building in Oklahoma City, which killed over 160 people, many of them small children, was a heinous act, an act whose depravity was exceeded only by the destruction on 9/11. The convictions of McVeigh and Nichols were preceded and followed by public clamors for the death penalty. Yet, because induced abortion has been sanitized, its heinous nature is conveniently kept from view. The media refer to proponents of abortion as "abortion rights" advocates. Imagine them referring as blithely to proponents of slavery as "slavery rights" advocates. Many people say, "I'm personally against abortion, but I wouldn't stop a woman from having one." Bumper stickers tell us, "If you don't like abortion, then don't have one." ("I'm personally against slavery, but I wouldn't stop someone from owning one"; "If you don't like slavery, then don't own a slave.")

I mentioned earlier that in the late sixties, many of us in the anti-abortion movement thought that by showing color slides and photographs of fetal development and aborted fetuses, we could change people's minds about abortion. It seemed reasonable to suppose that people would want to see what the real issues were in the debate. After all, the media, along with anti-war activists, thought it appropriate to show the American public film footage of U.S. planes dropping napalm on villages in Vietnam and the bodies of the civilian men, women and children left in its wake. And I remember seeing a television drama about Caryl Chessman's fight to avoid the gas chamber at San Quentin Prison that contained a powerful scene of a black man struggling against his guards as they strapped him into his death-chair. A powerfully built man, he screamed, "Mama!," like a child. But the audiences to whom I presented photographs of unborn and their mutilated bodies were not so ready to accept them as evidence. More than once, someone, usually a woman, would ask if these depictions of the unborn were life-size or were exaggerated for dramatic effect. In itself, a sensible question, but in that situation it was made in bad faith, for its intent was to discredit the validity of the photographs immediately. The size of the unborn appeared larger than in real life (or in real death), but that was only because the photographs were enlarged for display; the pictures were still to scale. I recall one occasion when a high school student walked straight up to me at the end of the class period in which I'd spoken and, making a great display of contempt, angrily crumpled up his copy of the photographs right in front of my face, threw it into the waste receptacle and stormed out of the room.

Now the striking thing about the above three depictions, the bombings in Vietnam, strapping the condemned man to the chair in the gas chamber, and aborted babies, is that the first two are not germane to the debate. The question of the morality of dropping bombs on the enemy is conceptually different from the question of the morality of bombing civilian areas; and even here one might justify such action as collateral damage according to the principle of double effect. If the U.S. planes were directly targeting noncombatants or reckless in their bombing of suspected military targets, that would be immoral. But even then that would not morally discredit the policy of dropping bombs on the enemy.

Given the heavy-handed anti-death penalty preachment of the aforementioned television show, it is clear that the scene of the man about to be executed was designed to create a sense of empathy with him among the viewers and a consequent sense of revulsion at the terror and inhumanity of the death penalty. I can think of several very good arguments against capital punishment, but the terror it strikes in the heart of the condemned is not one of them. In fact, it is irrelevant to the question of the death penalty's morality. We all rather suspected that is how you feel when you're about to be killed. The moral issue surrounding the death penalty is whether the state possesses the moral credentials to execute human beings.

Showing photographs of fetal development and abortion's victims is directly relevant to the question of the morality of abortion. For the overarching question is whether the fetus is a human being. From the instant that the pro-abortion movement got up its first head of steam, its spokespersons have labored relentlessly to create the image in the public mind of the unborn as subhuman. We used to hear references to "unborn children" or the "unborn baby." Those terms have been replaced with "fetus." Even though the word only refers to a stage of development (*fetus* in Latin means "offspring") – there are frog fetuses (polliwogs) and rabbit fetuses, but no one supposes that there are therefore sub-frogs and sub-rabbits – the purveyors of the term want us to forget that the being carried in a woman's uterus is a human being. There is not only a human *fetus* but also a human *infant*, a human *adolescent*, and a human *adult*. And they are all human beings.

As I describe in Chapter 5, once, when arguing for the humanity of the unborn before a seminar of graduate students in genetic counseling in the School of Public Health at the University of California at Berkeley, the professor challenged my reference to the embryo as a human being with the retort that it was only "a clump of cells." Not only is this misleading because it creates the impression that the cells are unorganized but, as I noted, you would be hard pressed to find the expression, "clump of cells," used in reference to the embryo in a book on embryology. And the media's addiction to the sensational produces a schizophrenic stance when reporting news stories on the unborn. When it's a story about abortion, they refer to the unborn as the "fetus;" when reporting a lifesaving, surgical intervention on the unborn, it is the "unborn baby."

Although I have long since abandoned the use of photographs or slides in my presentations on abortion, I continue to maintain that their use serves a valid purpose. They offer a vivid means of shaking people, who are used to allowing their life and thought to be dominated by socially created images, from the passive, unquestioning acceptance of the dehumanizing terms foisted on them by the pro-abortionists.

HOLDING THEIR FEET TO THE FIRE

When it comes to keeping an audience's attention on what abortion is all about, I must say the late Elizabeth Anscombe was in a class by herself. She was one of the most prominent philosopher's of our day. Holder of the Chair of Philosophy at Cambridge University until her retirement, Professor Anscombe wrote a number of influential works. At the St. Louis University abortion conference, she said in response to her co-panelist, a young assistant professor of theology at Boston College, "I wish the lady would stop using the word 'abortion' and say instead, 'the murder of conceived persons.'"

Another example of the sanitation of abortion occurred in spring, 1969, at the American Catholic Philosophical Association convention held in Chicago. A motion was put forward at the general business meeting for the Association to go on record as condemning the U.S. bombing of Cambodia. I objected from the floor that, as a scholarly association, we ought not to politicize ourselves, particularly when it is not clear that the bombing was immoral. I proposed instead that, if the Association were determined to go on record against something, how about condemning abortion. I pointed out that it would not be a political act in the sense that it does not support any political party or ideology but instead condemns what is intrinsically evil – the direct killing of the innocent. Guess what? Those present voted against my proposal in favor of condemning the bombing in Cambodia.

The terrorist attack in Oklahoma City and on 9/11 were terrible crimes. They horrified our nation with their indiscriminate murder of so many innocent people, among them small children. No doubt the profundity of their impact on us came also from the realization that, not even in America's heartland, are we safe from terrorist attack. That said, I nevertheless maintain that the murder of over one million unborn each year in this nation is, by its sheer magnitude, a more monstrous crime than both these outrages combined. To reiterate, the heartless deed of abortion has been institutionally sanitized. What McVeigh and Nichols did was perceived as all the more despicable because they were "losers." Induced abortion, even on a massive scale, is acceptable because the right kind of people do it and approve of it – our kind of people.

All of which reminds me of an episode in Steinbeck's *Grapes of Wrath*. As the family prepares to leave the dustbowl for California, they must buy automobile parts to repair their broken down truck and in the process, find that some merchants are cheating them. That discovery leads the grandfather to observe: if we steal something from the storeowner, we're thieves; but if he knowingly sells us a defective tire, that's not dishonesty, it's good business. Assassinating members of society is murder; but deliberately killing the unborn is not murder; it's the exercise of a Constitutional right to privacy.

The pro-life movement is not the first movement for social reform that has attracted violent supporters; they are bad companions, indeed. But if they are worse than the abortionists and their supporters, that is only because the latter operate within the law whereas the former do not. The "respectable, law abiding" abortionists deliberately kill millions of innocent human beings, usually for profit. You might call the abortionists "good citizens," but as Aristotle noted in the *Politics* and the Nuremberg Court noted in 1946, that is not the same as being a "good human being." When convicted killer of the Jews, Adolph Eichmann, stood before the Israeli High Tribunal in 1961, he argued that German law demanded what he did to the Jews. The tribunal responded by saying that he was correct in saying that the laws of Germany required the starvation and execution of the Jews, but went on to remark that he should have known, nevertheless, that what he had done against innocent human beings was immoral.

CHAPTER FIVE

THE HIDDEN CHILD

"'What's a knight errant?', asked the young woman.

'Are you such a newcomer to this world that you don't know this?', replied Sancho Panza. 'Then learn, sister, that a knight errant is something that can be summed up in two words: whipping-boy and emperor. One day he's the most unfortunate creature in the world and the neediest, and the next he has two or three crowns with which to set up his squire as king over as many kingdoms.'"

The Adventures of Don Quixote, Pt. I, Ch. XVI

Sometimes the most successful way to hide something is not to hide it at all. In Edgar Allan Poe's story, *The Purloined Letter,* the chief of police fails, despite all his experience and skill, to find a stolen letter. He and his detectives search in vain because they assume the letter, being so crucial a piece of evidence, would be cached in some out of the way place when all along it remains in plain view in the card rack on the wall where the thief had placed it.

In abortion debates, the unborn child, it turns out, is hard to find, even though you would suppose that it would be the immediate center of attention. That should be as obvious as the letter on the card rack in Poe's story. For the moral justification for induced abortion depends more on the answer to the question, "Is induced abortion the deliberate killing of a human being?" than on any other consideration. And what, after all, is so odd about saying that induced abortion kills a child or a baby instead of a fetus? "Fetus" denotes a stage of development; it doesn't mean that the unborn is subhuman, though that is just what the pro-abortionists hoped for when they persuaded the media and then the medical profession and finally the people to say "fetus" instead of "child" or "baby". But if a term indicating a stage of mammalian development is to be the term of choice, then why not, in the name of consistency, adopt a policy of insisting that babies be referred to as "infants," children as "adolescents," and mature humans as "adults"? Maybe that's just what we'll do when the death peddlers get around to legalizing the killing of children and adults.

When I first got into the abortion debate, I had to get used to the remarkable, but under the circumstances hardly curious, fact that pro-abortionists religiously make a point of sidestepping the central, all-important issue. Hardly any of my debate opponents have been willing to address the matter of whether the fetus is a human being. I say this is not curious because the evidence on the positive side of the question overwhelms any evidence that you could muster on the negative side. What my opponents deliver instead are pleas for the liberation of women from the oppressive society and so forth. The fact that they have almost always come from outside the academic community probably explains their evasive tactics. Being more practical and activist than theoretical and reflective, their commitment is to persuade their listeners to support legalized abortion on request rather than to delve into the foundational ethical and ontological considerations.

Had my opponents been professors, especially philosophy professors, they surely would have addressed the status of the fetus. In the first chapter I cited authors, all academics, and their works as examples of that focus. In my thirty-six years debating abortion, the only opponent I can recall who met the issue head-on is Mary Ann Warren of San Francisco State University. As I noted earlier, she is a gradualist or developmentalist insofar as she admits that the fetus is human but denies that it is a person. Several years back, I debated a Unitarian minister at University High School in San Francisco. Although he expressed agreement with my claim that all the evidence supported the position that the fetus is a human being, he went on to describe "the professor" (me) as naïve. Why? Because women, including teen-age girls, are going to have abortions anyway, so we ought to ensure that the procedure is legal and safe. This position can hardly be characterized as meeting the moral issue head on. I'm convinced that my audiences over the years would have been far better informed on what is at stake in elective abortion if my opponents had been other philosophy professors, like Mary Ann Warren. But you debate the opponents you're given.

My wife, Maryann, brought one example of this characteristic evasion of the issue home to me. For five consecutive years, I had been invited each spring semester to address the graduate students in a seminar on genetic counseling in the School of Public Health at the University of California at Berkeley. It was a select program that accepted no more than eight applicants a year from all over the nation. I don't recall the students in the seminar room numbering more than eight or nine on any of my visits, so it was always what you might call a cheek by jowl encounter. Their reaction to my anti-abortion presentation was predictable in light of the program's slant – counseling couples on whether they should have an abortion. On one particular occasion, Maryann joined me in the seminar room as an observer. For two hours she sat silently, listening and watching. When it was over, she said to me as soon as we left the room, "That was the most emotionally intense two hours I have ever experienced." She went on to point out a remarkable polarity: despite the fact that my presentation was rational, to wit, logically coherent and grounded in empirical evidence and accessible texts, and despite the fact that those students were supposedly among the brightest, their reaction was totally emotional and vindictive insofar as they did no more then express contempt and ridicule with occasional personal attacks on me. At one point in the seminar, the professor referred to the zygote as "a clump of cells." So far as I know, one searches the scientific literature in vain for the category "clump" as a stage of mammalian development.

My debate opponents from the American Civil Liberties Union have taken a different tack. Over the years, I've faced a number of them. The first one I debated on an hour-long, live call-in TV show and a year or two later at the Hasting School of Law in San Francisco. Her argument about the fetus was the same in both meetings: the question of whether the fetus is a human being is a religious issue and is thus, by definition, a matter for personal belief; therefore it cannot be subject to public policy or law. Another one whom I debated several times at U.C. Berkeley, employed a theatrical tactic. She would ask the audience of 700 students:

"How many think the fetus is a human being?" Hands would be raised. Then she would ask: How many think that it is not a human being?" Hands would be raised. Finally, she would ask: "How many aren't sure?" Hands would be raised. First looking in my direction and then to the audience, she would confidently announce, "See, the question is too much in doubt to come under the law; it has to be left up to the individual's conscience."

I suppose I have debated representatives of Planned Parenthood more often than anyone else. They seem to prefer the emotional, tug-at-your-heartstrings approach. Personal testimony is big with them. For example, one of my Planned Parenthood opponents told the audience that she got pregnant during her undergraduate years and had an abortion. (Given her age at the time of the debate, I could only infer that it was an illegal abortion.) She justified it by saying that it was the wrong time in her life to have a child. She had nobody to turn to and would have had to drop out of college. Thanks to the abortion, she was able to graduate; when she was more mature, she married and had children and now finds her grand-child so adorable and loveable, etc. The genius (evil though it be) of this form of "argument" is that it appeals to the audience's sense of enlight-ened practicality: "Look how happily things turned out as a result of the abortion; if I had had the baby out of wedlock as a teenager, who knows what my predicament would be today. Besides, see what a nice, loving grandmother I am."

What her listeners may not have detected was what her tale implied: she aborted her baby because it was in the way; if her grandchild had been that baby, then ....?

NOW representatives have also been frequent opponents. Their argu-ments for abortion are basically the same as those advanced by Planned Parenthood – reproductive freedom, personal testimony to the redemp-tive powers of abortion as a young woman, etc.

Another form of dodging the issue of the fetus is the question, inevi-tably directed to an anti-abortion debater, "What if the pregnancy is due to rape?" The idea being that nobody with humanitarian instincts would dream of making a woman bear and nurture a child conceived in rape. Here is the answer I always give: " Rape is a terrible crime and the victim's anguish must be multiplied many times when it results in pregnancy. But given what I've argued about the nature of the fetus, that it is a human being, how could I justify abortion, even when the pregnancy is due to rape? For then besides one innocent victim, the woman, we add a second innocent victim, the child. Although conceived by a despicable, criminal act, the child has committed no crime; yet by destroying it, we, in effect, punish him or her for the crime of the rapist. If, as I argue, it is always wrong to deliberately kill an innocent human being, then it is morally unjustifiable to abort the fetus even when it is conceived by rape."

STAYING FOCUSED

This is not an easy thing to do, mainly because abortion supporters, like so many advocates on the left of an issue, have a taste for the *ad hominem* argument: they shift attention from the topic of debate to your character or personality. This, of course, is another common way of ducking the question, "Is the fetus a human being?". What makes it so effective as a distraction is our natural, even reflexive, urge to defend ourselves. I've found two good ways of replying, depending on circumstances.

The first way is to use a little humor to make clear immediately to all present that the question or comment is out of place. My only caveat is first to make sure the audience is in the mood for humor: "Thank you for shifting attention from the topic we came here to discuss to my personality. Vanity tempts me to go along with you and focus the discussion on my life, my moods, and myself. But I fear I'd only bore you without adding anything to the discussion. So, if you don't mind, I'd prefer to confine my comments to the topic of abortion."

The second way is to meet the *ad hominem* head-on and put its author on the defensive. Recently at U.C. Berkeley, a student in the audience indignantly asked me, "Who are you to come over here and tell women what to do with their bodies?" I replied: "In the first place, I didn't solicit this gig; the people who run this course invited me over. In the second place, I find your question a bit curious, especially in the open forum of a university. Who is so self-righteous as to get upset by any question or even criticism of conduct, law, or public policy? Education, especially at the university level, would be impossible if we did not rely on Socrates' dictum, 'Let the argument lead where it may and we shall follow.' If we come to a debate seeking the truth, we should welcome criticism of our views. If you tell me that you disagree with my position, I want to know why. If the reasons you advance for your disagreement show me the error of my position, then I should thank you for enlightening me. If, on the contrary, I'm able to answer your criticism to my satisfaction, then I should also be grateful for having had the opportunity to vindicate my position before the bar of reason. If I don't find your argument persuasive and yet cannot refute it, then that tells me that I need to take a closer look at my own reasons. In any event, it seems to me that one can only benefit from listening to arguments for a position with which one may be in disagreement. Thus, I confess I fail to see the relevance, especially in a university setting, of asking, 'Who are you to come over here and tell women what to do with their bodies?'"

My experience has been that the most important way to ensure your focus for the debate is to work on what athletes call "the inner game." You must walk onto the debate stage confident that you'll deliver an articulate, persuasive account of your position. That requires two things. First, prepare, prepare, and prepare. You must cast your argument into effective form; it must have a cutting edge. Don't try to say everything you think should be said. That will only blunt its cutting edge and rob your argument of its power. By trying to say too many things, you diffuse the energy of your presentation, with the result that you've lessened its impact on your audience. Ask yourself, "What thought on abortion do I wish to leave my audience with?" For me, it has always been, "Abortion is the direct killing of an innocent human being; if you don't find the evidence for that conclusive, it's still obviously preponderant and persuasive enough to support the conclusion that, at the very least, abortion is most probably the direct killing of an innocent human being; therefore the willingness to destroy the fetus is the willingness to destroy an innocent human being." (See Chapter 6) On this point I'm dogged; like a bulldog, I refuse to be pulled off it. If my opponent or a member of the audience manages to pull me off with questions or objections about something else, I reply in such a way that I'm able to fasten back on my point. I want to do everything I can to make sure that my listeners never think the same way about abortion again.

What about your opponent's argument, or what you anticipate it to be? Make sure you understand that argument and then cast it in its strongest form before formulating your objections to it. If you create a "straw man" out of your opponent's argument, you'll leave yourself open to a strong rebuttal. Besides, you should only enter a debate in the spirit of truth seeking and that means you must treat opposing arguments in an objective and open-minded fashion.

The next step in getting prepared is rehearsal. I recite my presentation over and over in my mind and aloud when alone in my office or automobile. It helps if you can give your presentation before some friends or family members. They often spot weaknesses in it that you don't see. Successful boxers "listen to their corners." They know that their trainers and managers see things they're doing in the boxing ring that they themselves don't see. Let your friendly audience tell you how you're doing.

The second thing you must do for the "inner game" is to "psych yourself up." Knowing that you've mastered your presentation will give you confidence, but more has to be done. Knowing what we are going to say is a matter of intellect. But we're not pure intellects; the emotions, the passions, and the will must be prepared as well. I tell myself over and over and over that when I debate, I'll be articulate, confident and cogent. I've become a great believer in self-hypnosis or self-programming. As the day of the debate gets closer, I find myself increasingly preoccupied by it. Right up until the debate itself I continue to work on my "inner game," to "psych myself up." For that reason I always drive to the debate alone. Often one or more of my students will ask to ride with me to the event, but I inevitably refuse. I explain to them that I need that time for preparation and focus.

There is a massive difference between going into a debate with confidence and going there with arrogance or self-complacency. Confidence has to do with your sense that you've thoroughly prepared and that you can give a persuasive account of your position. I always feel more assured when I'm a little scared. Fear tells you not to underestimate your opponent. I always prepare for a debate by supposing that my opponent is very intelligent, able and learned. That makes me prepare all the harder. Fear is good; panic is bad. But if you've readied yourself and possess a realistic assessment of your ability to speak and handle objections and even personal attacks, you've no reason to panic. When I first get on the debate stage, I casually survey my audience while breathing diaphragmatically and slowly. Not only does this type of breathing have a calming effect, I've found that it lends a richness and steadiness to the speaking voice.

Sometimes external forces in your life make it difficult to gain focus for the debate. Once I accepted an abortion debate one day before the event. Besides having next to no time to work on the "inner game," I was engrossed in writing an important public lecture on a somewhat different topic for another university. Consequently, my performance in the debate lacked the force and sharpness of my other debates, not to mention displaying tentativeness in my overall manner.

On another occasion, I had plenty of time to get ready, but there was a persistent problem in my life that kept me in a perpetual state of distraction. During a debate against an ACLU attorney held at the University of California's Hastings School of Law in San Francisco, my lack of focus showed up in the form of inattentiveness and mental lethargy. In the course of answering a question from the audience, my opponent said that the DNA code in the zygote didn't make it a human being because it was only a "blueprint" for a human being. Had I been alert, I would've jumped in at that point and challenged her misuse of the blueprint metaphor. I would've remarked that if blueprints were parallel to zygotes, we would have blueprints that grow into houses. That kind of timely rejoinder can score a lot of points, especially when you're arguing that the fetus is a human being and your opponent – typical of ACLU debaters – wants to get that issue out of the discussion as quickly as possible. But the reality is I didn't jump in and say it, so my pro-abortion opponent scored the points.

THE IMPORTANCE OF NOT "WINNING"

John Brodie, a former quarterback for the San Francisco 49ers, once observed, "The fans are with you, win or draw." People may agree, "It's not who wins or loses, but how the game is played that counts," but the fact is that everyone loves a winner. Is that the way to enter a debate? Go in to win? If you do, you will eventually do what some politicians, lawyers, and college athletic directors do: lie and cheat. The reason directors of college athletic programs are sometimes in trouble with the NCAA is that they are not hired to teach young men and women to play well and fair but to win.

At times this "debating not to win" rule can be hard to follow. Once when debating an ACLU attorney, I asserted that the U.S. Supreme Court in *Roe v. Wade* did not address the question of the personhood of the fetus. Here my memory failed me. My opponent insisted that the court did address it; when I challenged him to show me where in the court document that would be found, he said the document was in his briefcase, but it would be hard to find now among all his papers. I interpreted that as an evasion: either the document wasn't with him or he wasn't sure it did address the topic of personhood. Several weeks later, while pouring over *Roe v. Wade* in preparation for my bioethics class, I found that he was right and I was wrong. In one place, Justice Blackmun writes, "...the word 'person,' as used in the Fourteenth Amendment, does not include the unborn," and in another place, "...the unborn have never been recognized in the law as persons in the whole sense." I should have sent my opponent a note admitting my error. Given the number of years that have since gone by, I wonder if there is a statute of limitations covering apologies.

Another time I'd accepted an invitation to give a public lecture on abortion at Sonoma State University near Santa Rosa, which is about a ninety-minute drive north from San Francisco. The hall was filled and it seemed that the pro-abortionists were all seated on one side of the aisle and the anti-abortionists on the other. I had been warned that a campus club of militant feminists would be there. What I was not prepared for was their constant interruptions during my lecture. The moderator was an undergraduate who was totally unequal to the task of controlling them. Their intrusiveness unraveled me. For example, instead of saying "conception," I was apparently repeatedly saying "conceptualization." (I must have thought I was teaching my theory of knowledge class.) When one of the feminists corrected me, I responded by saying that "conceptualization" could be used as a synonym for "conception." I can't be sure what my motives were in saying that; in retrospect, I have the vague sense that in my disorientation produced by the constant interruptions, I wasn't sure I'd made a mistake but at the same time felt that something was wrong with that use of the word. I wish I had simply accepted the correction and proceeded with what I came to say. I think that a gracious acknowledgment in cases like that score a lot more points with the audiences than a defensive response.

Some opponents are so adept at making your position seem silly to the audience that you know from the start you'll be swimming upstream for the entire debate. A case in point occurred six or seven years ago at an upscale private high school in San Francisco. My opponent represented Planned Parenthood. He was a thirtyish, plump man with glasses and mustache wearing a rumpled blue suit. The impression of a rather mild, non-threatening person was only strengthened when he told me before the debate that he'd never done this kind of thing before and didn't know much about debating. As it turned out, he was the debate equivalent of the pool hall hustler, the guy who lulls you into a false sense of confidence by letting you win a couple of games of billiards, so he can trick you into playing him for some big money.

When the debate got underway, I quickly found out that he was intelligent, mentally quick and knew a lot more about abortion than I'd have guessed. In professional boxing, an important knack is that of "stealing" the round from your opponent by a flurry of punches in the final twenty seconds. Even though he may have, in fact, won the round, what stays in the minds of the three judges is your flurry, so they award the round to you. My opponent had the knack of timing his statements in such a way that I didn't have time to reply; another question or comment from the audience had to be addressed. I found this especially annoying because his representations of my position or of the facts were, if not false, at least caricatures. For example, with regard to my assertion that from the moment of conception we have a human being, he replied: "When I eat scrambled eggs in the restaurant, I'm not eating chicken." The adolescent audience burst into an approving laughter. With that the debate ended and he got the last word. I'm sure it seemed to many of them that he'd succeeded in reducing my central thesis to absurdity. If only there had been time to point out that a huge difference separates eggs that are fertilized from eggs that are unfertilized. But that would have to wait for another time.

Debaters committed to giving witness to the truth do not, as I observed above, seek to "win" and that's why they don't care about manipulating or finessing their audience or in diminishing their opponent, either by ridicule or vilification. Their commitment to the truth creates a freedom in them: because they want the truth above all else, they're always ready to admit the error of their own position should the evidence so indicate. And if the evidence so indicates, they are ultimately not disappointed, for they have reached what they sought, after all — the truth.

When you're facing an opponent who wants only to "win," you might want to remind yourself that audience manipulation did not die with the Greek sophists. In Plato's dialogue, *Gorgias*, the famed sophist, Gorgias, boasts that his oratory is so persuasive that he and a physician could petition the assembly of legislators for a license to practice medicine and they would confer it on him instead of the physician. Socrates replies by telling Gorgias that the reason his oratory is so persuasive is that he flatters his audience's tastes. Imagine, Socrates continues, a pastry chef and a health trainer arguing for acceptance of their respective diets before a jury of children. Which menu, Socrates asks, will get the vote? The pastry chef's, of course. The reason is that his food flatters the taste of the children; it gives them what they *want* to eat rather than what they *need* to eat. Similarly, he tells Gorgias, his oratory wins the audience over to his side by telling them what they *want* to hear instead of what they *need* to hear.

THE POWER OF REASON AND DECENCY

If you offer your audience rational arguments and show that you've done your homework on the subject and if you are not self-righteous or arrogant, you will reach the people who have come to the debate with an open mind; you'll even reach some among the closed-minded. Take a look at the following samples of the letters I've received from the students at the University of California, Berkeley who are responsible for organizing and supervising the course, "Social, Ethical and Political Issues in Health and Medicine," to which I'm regularly invited to debate.

> September 20, 1993
>
> Dear Dr. Dennehy,
>
> I would like to take this opportunity to thank you for

speaking to our IDS 130 class about abortion. Your arguments are enlightening. This is the third time I have heard
you speak on the topic, and your discussion is more convincing every semester. You are very clear in your reasons for being anti-abortion and this clarity is refreshing.

Sincerely,

[Signed]...

Assistant Coordinator

February 28, 1995

Dear Dr. Dennehy,

We...appreciate your willingness to once again take time
out of your busy schedule to share your views with our
class. I have seen your presentation several times, and I
am always impressed by your logical construction of argument. Your presentation style is refreshingly clear and
always encourages our class to pursue such clarity in the
justification of their own views, whatever they may be.
This time the debate was particularly heated, yet you
maintained your composure and remained focused on
your principle (*sic*) arguments. Your professionalism was
much admired by the class.

Thank you for your participation in our program. We
hope to be working again with you in the future.

Sincerely,

[Signed]...

Assistant Coordinator

January 14, 1997

Dear Dr. Dennehy:

We are writing this letter to thank you for the informa-
tive lecture you presented to our health issues class last
semester. As always, your talk provided an interesting and

invaluable perspective for discussion of the abortion issue with our students. Many of our students were impressed with your lecture and impacted by your scenarios
and statistics. We have also included some letters written
to you by our students.

As a coordinator it is often difficult finding anti–abortion speakers who present academic and thought provoking arguments against abortion. In fact, your well
considered, reasonable presentation generated the most
discussion in our classes that week. Thank you for your
numerous lectures over the years and for your continued
support of our program. Your flexibility in accepting various speaking partners is greatly appreciated. We hope that
your remain involved with the program for future lectures to benefit students....

Sincerely,

[Signed] ...

IDS 130 Co-Coordinator

You can't get through to some students because they are either dog-
matic, air-headed or defensive; some are defensive because they are insecure about their own pro-choice position and others because they've had
abortions and can't admit to themselves what they've done. When I debate abortion at the University of California at Berkeley my aim is to
speak in such a way that the young men and women in my audience will
never think the same way about abortion again. Even though they may
claim to reject my arguments and in some cases, scoff at them, I remain
confident that I've planted seeds in their minds that will germinate over
time. We must not forget that the vast majority of them have been intellectually victimized by years of brainwashing from the media and the
schooling system, so that by the time you address them their minds have
been saturated by materialistic and hedonistic doctrines tricked out in
emotionally laden clichés. Despite their self-flattery, they are the dogma-
tists. From time to time the Berkeley students who are in my audience
send me letters, saying that that was the first time they'd ever heard a
rational, as opposed to a religious or emotional, argument against abor-

tion. March 18th, 2002, marked my 30th semester debating abortion there before classes of 700 students. This has enabled me to accumulate a pretty reliable sampling of their attitudes over the years.

Sometimes debates have two speakers for each side. In getting through to your audience, the importance of having a good debate-partner cannot be emphasized too much. Some debaters are either incompetent or heavy-handed to the point that you don't need any opponents: they do more harm than good. A case in point is the attorney I describe in Chapter 4, under the heading, "WITH BOORISH PARTNERS, DO WE NEED OPPONENTS?" He was so aggressive, so intent on saying everything he thought should be said, that he took up almost the entire time allotted for all the speakers to respond to questions and comments and thereby alienated the audience of students.

Another time my partner, who was head of education for a state pro-life group, was downright incompetent. Rather than appealing to arguments and evidence, she was anecdotal, citing, for example, a case in Florida where the abortionist was so feckless about sanitation that his dog followed him about the clinic licking up the blood that spilled on the floor from the abortions. The audience expressed its disapproval of this tack with audible groans and laughter. To make matters worse, when asked what her position was on abortion for rape victims, she began her reply by asking the questioner whether we were talking about "true rape." I understand the distinction she had in mind, but it is massively impolitic to talk like that to an audience of university women. The audience's expressed indignation drove that point home to her.

Several years ago, I had what might be described, in the *patois* of the times, as an "up close and personal" experience of how women's denial to themselves about their abortions produces such strong resistance to discussion of the subject as to lead to disruption in the classroom. I was teaching the course in bioethics that I taught every semester. The course always gets a fair representation of nursing students. In this particular semester many of the nursing majors were in their thirties or early forties. That was because the university then had an accelerated nursing program that permitted people with a bachelor's degree in some other field to get a nursing degree in fifteen months of intensive course-work. As always, the course addressed the standard bioethical topics, including abortion. Three things deserve attention here: first, having had the course syllabus, the students knew from the start that abortion would be discussed; second, the topic of abortion was given no more time and attention than the others; third, although I present my own position on abortion, as I do on all the topics, I make it abundantly clear that the students will not be required to accept or defend my positions in the examinations and that the assigned readings consist of representative positions on both sides of the topics and it is a knowledge of these for which the student will be held responsible. Nevertheless, when we got to abortion, one student in particular began disruptive behavior. She would turn around and proceed to talk for protracted periods to the student seated immediately behind her while I was lecturing; when she wasn't doing that, she would lay her head on the desk, pretending to sleep, but made sure that she'd made enough commotion in finding a comfortable position to draw my attention to her.

I did manage to get her undivided attention one day when I mentioned in passing the percentage of late term abortions performed annually according to the abortion surveillance report regularly put out by the Centers for Disease Control. She objected that it was a very small percentage of all the abortions; I replied that, even so, 0.5 % of one million is not a number to be ignored, especially if you're talking about killing human beings. Several lectures later, she said aloud, "We don't want to hear any more about abortion; most of us here have had abortions and we've heard all that before." Then another student raised her hand and said that she would rather hear me lecture on the problems of health care delivery in the United States. I explained that I hadn't finished with the topic yet, but after a third student objected, I made it clear that the course would go on as set forth in the syllabus and if they didn't like it they could see the dean. That they did, but he backed me up. Not only did he say that what I chose to lecture on was an academic freedom issue; he also reminded them that students did not dictate curriculum to the College of Arts and Sciences. Failing there, they went to the ombudsman, but to no avail. The disruptive conduct continued to the course's end. About two weeks after the course ended, I found under my office door a copy of the Centers for Disease Control's abortion surveillance report, on the cover of which was written in pen: "Merry Christmas, Dr. Dennehy in the hopes that you use these statistics wisely, TRUTHFULLY and in CON-

TEXT. Just the facts, man. – some of your bio-ethics students." (Students' emphasis)

This note is only another indication of something that people active in the abortion debate are doubtless familiar with: Owing to the impoverishment of their position, pro-abortionists frequently adopt the tactic of trying to discredit their opponents by exaggerating some statement made by the latter to the point of distorting its relevance to the debate. By focusing on the small percentage of later term abortions and ignoring how many abortions out of a million that amounts to, my pro-abortionist students wished to create the impression that my statement misrepresented the facts.

DEBATING "EXPERTS"

It's only natural to stand in awe of experts, especially scientists. So facing a pro-abortion scientist can be intimidating. When that happens, it's helpful to ask what your opponent's area of expertise exactly is since the evidence against abortion is more commonsensical and philosophical than scientific. My experience has been that when a scientist argues that the fetus is not a human being, he is, more often than not, doing philosophy – and ineptly at that – but dressing it in the clothes of science. For example, when I first started debating the topic, I found myself against a biochemist at Berkeley. At one point he asked me, "Why are you so concerned about the fetus and not about what happens to the sperm or the egg?" I asked in turn, "Are you saying that the fetus is not importantly different from either the sperm or the egg?" "I am," he answered. This left me momentarily speechless; he was so obviously wrong, yet I couldn't think of how to show why. Then it came to me and I asked him: "Would you say, then, that water is not importantly different from hydrogen and oxygen?" It was his turn to be speechless; then he responded rather feebly, "That's different."

A few years back, I debated an embryologist at U.C., Berkeley. I went into the event with butterflies in my stomach; he was, after all, not only a physician but also a Ph.D. in embryology from Oxford in addition to being a major player in family planning for Third World countries. Everything I knew about the human embryo was on a need-to-know-basis. "This guy," I thought over and over again, "will destroy me. He'll expose my ignorance in no time." But instead of talking like a scientist, he proceeded to argue by appealing to fallacious arguments. They were classic fallacies, the kind you discuss in a freshman logic class. For example, he tried to identify the anti-abortionists with dictators and fascists by saying things like, "Hitler was against abortion; so was Idi Amin." When I said he didn't talk scientifically, I mean it: "I can," he continued, "tell the difference between a three-day old embryo and an eight month old fetus." (Gee, doc, don't get too technical on us here.)

When my turn for rebuttal came, I called the audience's attention to the point that not only is it irrelevant to the issue of the morality of abortion to cite who was for or against abortion, but that, as a matter of fact, Hitler was against abortion for Aryan women but not for Jews, Gypsies and Slavs. My opponent's second point, I noted, rested on the fallacy of arguing from appearances. A three-day old embryo doesn't look like an eight-month-old fetus, but you can't infer from that appearance that the embryo is not a human being while the fetus is, just as you can't infer that the sun is smaller than the earth because that's the way it appears. That was the substance of the embryologist's argument. During the question period that followed, it was clear that the audience, regardless of their individual positions on abortion, were not impressed with it.

Sometimes it's not the expertise of your opponent that lays you low but your own bumbling. A couple of years ago, I'd agreed to debate a trial lawyer from downtown here at the University of San Francisco. I went into the affair with the assumption that she would be self-possessed and sharp because those are the kinds of qualities, it seemed to me, that trial lawyers needed. But although she was clearly intelligent and self-possessed, she never recovered from her initial mistake. Maybe she thought to ingratiate herself with the audience of a Catholic university by identifying her position on the status of the fetus with that of Thomas Aquinas who taught, following the Aristotelian biology, that it took forty days for the male fetus to get a human soul and eighty days for the female. When my turn at the podium came, all I had to do was

begin by calling attention to the curious fact of someone in the twentieth century arguing on the basis of the biology of the thirteenth century and then proceed to present the mainstream views on the fetus
from contemporary embryology. Returning to the podium, she confessed her embarrassment at making such a basic mistake, but then immediately held up a full-page advertisement in the *New York Times*, signed
by 160 scientists, stating that the fetus was not a human being. She had
come prepared. I'd walked right into that one by committing a *genetic*
fallacy. You do this, not by evaluating the argument itself, but by citing
the supposed inadequacies of the conditions that spawned it or by claiming that those conditions no longer obtain. All my opponent had to do
was to produce examples of contemporary biologists who claimed that
the fetus was not a human being.

Although I was able to reply that the advertisement was a typical
case of scientists waxing philosophical while maintaining the aura of
scientific authority, it was clear that my appeal to contemporary science
had taken a big hit. In my thirty-odd years of classroom teaching and
public speaking, I have learned that audiences, even a supposedly sophisticated gathering of university students, are impressionistic; and my
opponent had just made a big impression. Many of those present would
infer that the scientific community must be divided on the issue and
thus that the question of the status of the fetus is up for grabs. The more
acute among them might have been able to distinguish between *what
some scientists say* and *what science says*. But you always fear that many
members of your audience are more impressionistic than acute.

I said above that she never recovered from her initial mistake. What I
meant was that she was always on the defensive, waiting to be embar-
rassed again. And just because the argument against abortion is more
commonsensical and philosophical than scientific, I was able to keep
the audience's attention on the malice of directly killing a fetus – to the
tune of one million legal abortions a year in the United States alone –
when doubt is expressed about its being human. If you justify killing a
fetus on the premise that there is uncertainty over whether it's a human
being, that is nothing less than expressing the willingness to kill a human being.

Almost a full month after the debate, a copy of the following letter,
written to the president of the university, came into my hands. My

opponent's colleague wrote it on Law Office letterhead:

> April 20, 1994
>
> Dear Father Schlegel:
>
> On the evening of March 24, 1994, I attended a debate on your campus concerning whether abortion should remain safe and legal in the United States. Attorney…, President of the Northern Chapter of the California Abortion Rights Action League (CARAL) debated Dr. Dennehy, who is apparently a bioethics professor at USF, on that issue. I would like to voice my concern concerning two aspects of that debate.
>
> The first aspect was Dr. Dennehy's demeanor and use of terms "murderers" and "vampires" in reference to doctors that perform abortions and women who undergo abortions. I felt that for a person in Dr. Dennehy's position, a professor at USF, to use such terms in a scholarly debate was inappropriate. Dr. Dennehy also referred to perfusion experiments on carbohydrate metabolism wherein fetal heads were supposedly used. He provided no facts or documentation on such "experiments" but just suggested the morbid image of defenseless fetuses being decapitated by "vampires." Such sensationalism and propaganda, especially from a person with the authority of a USF professor, does not belong in an institute of higher learning.....
>
> I would very much appreciate your responding to the concerns expressed in this letter.
>
>
> Very truly yours,
>
> [Signed]

[The second aspect of the writer's concern was literature claiming a link between abortion and breast cancer distributed by "Students United for Life." The writer said the literature provided no evidence for the claim and was misleading and dangerous to young women.]

The writer sent copies of her letter to the editors of *The San Francisco Chronicle* and *The San Francisco Examiner*, though neither published it. The fact that the letter was written almost a month after the debate suggests that the author — whose behavior toward my opponent at the debate showed that they were colleagues and even friends — was more than just annoyed with the way things went. My guess, especially since she sent copies of the letter to our local newspapers, is that their speaker's "second-best" performance festered within them until finally they felt compelled to write a letter of protest.

If the letter had been written — even one month later — only to complain about the alleged defects in the information of the handouts, it could be seen as reasonable behavior. But its opening paragraph was against things I'd allegedly said in the debate — and that is unreasonable behavior. Suppose I had called abortionists "murderers" and "vampires." So? That would have been reasonable speech since I hold that the unborn is a human being. On that premise what could abortionists be if not "murderers"?

While I can't be sure I didn't accuse doctors who perform abortions of being "murderers," I'd be surprised if I did, for I scrupulously avoid any kind of name-calling in my debates. I did use the word "murder" with regard to abortion, but in the following way. I argued that the abortion controversy in the twentieth century has proved to be a bone in society's throat the way the slavery issue was a bone in its throat in the nineteenth century. As an example of this, I cited the California State Supreme Court ruling, *People v. Davis*, in 1993, that a third party who kills a nonviable fetus may be charged with murder, but hastened to add that that ruling didn't nullify a woman's *Constitutional* right to an abortion. The question I put forth in the debate was this: since it is the same unborn who is killed in both cases, why isn't it also murder when a woman has an abortion? I can't be sure, but I might even have gone so far as to say something like, "If it's murder when a third part kills the fetus, then it's murder when the woman kills her fetus." I might have, but I don't think so.

About the charge that I called the doctors "vampires," I was referring to fetal transplants for the treatment of adult ailments like diabetes and Parkinson's disease. My reasoning being that the defining characteristic of the vampire in both eastern and western culture is draining energy and life from the victim for one's own benefit.

Second, I might not have produced evidence of the severed fetal heads kept alive by perfusion, but I had a photocopy of the magazine article about it among my debate materials that evening. The magazine, *Medical World News*, reported that a team of Finnish and American scientists conducted an experiment in Helsinki in which they severed the heads of 12 pre-viable fetuses obtained by abdominal hysterotomy at 12 to 20 weeks gestation and kept the heads alive to test their capacity to metabolize sugar substitutes. When I go to debate abortion, I don't leave home without it.

My concern about debating an "expert," was in this case misplaced. I'm sure my opponent was an expert attorney and very capable in the courtroom. But that didn't make her an expert debater on abortion. If she had handled herself more competently in the debate, I suspect there would have been no letter at all.

NO MORE "MR. NICE GUY"

I'd agreed to a radio debate with a member of a woman's group from San Francisco State University. She showed up with another woman and when it was time to go on the air, she asked me if I minded if her friend participated with her. The show's host had no objection, so it was up to me to say "yes" or "no." I didn't like the idea of two-against-one, but, not wishing to seem petty or uncongenial, I agreed. I didn't realize until we started broadcasting what a blunder I'd made: I'd given my opponents two-thirds of the time to talk, leaving myself one-third. The evening was not without its consolations, however. It was a call-in show. A woman caller's inability to conceal her anguish gained much more for my side of the debate than I lost by the two-against-one speaking arrangement. She was in the process of telling the radio audience and me how good her abortion had been for her, when she broke into sobs and grew silent without ever hanging up. She was giving the pro-abortion party line perfectly; the only thing was she didn't believe it. It was not her anguish that consoled me but her inability to conceal it was a stronger argument against abortion than anything I could have said.

On October 6, 1997, I'd agreed to debate a woman from Planned Parenthood at U.C., Berkeley. Just before it began, the moderator asked if we wanted to debate or simply give presentations on our respective positions. My opponent said she didn't want to debate because that would be too hostile and aggressive. Although the moderator and I both made clear to her that a debate didn't have to be either, we finally settled on just giving presentations. Apparently she said she didn't want to go first; so the moderator asked me to give the first presentation and I complied. That was a huge mistake on my part, for which I have no excuse; I've been around long enough to know better. Here's what happened.

After I delivered my lecture, she began hers by rebutting me. So the event was in fact a debate, but with one big difference: I had no opportunity to rebut her or to reply to her criticisms since it was not a formal debate. Had I been a little tough-minded, I would have insisted before going to the podium either that each of us has the chance to rebut the other and to make closing comments or that my opponent give the first presentation. I still can't figure out why I agreed to the arrangement.

TUNING IN TO THE AUDIENCE

The late philosopher and mathematician, Bertrand Russell, said in his essay, "How I Write," that in general he never used a big word where a small one would do and that he avoided using jargon whenever possible. That made a big impression on me, for Russell, a Nobel Prize winner in literature, wrote in a marvelously clear and simple style. I've found that, as a general principle, when I think that my presentation against abortion is too simple or unsophisticated, it's just perfect for my listeners. I'm not being patronizing or snobbish. It's just that it's easy to overlook how far you've traveled in your own thinking and research from the level of the ordinary person. It took some time for me to realize that you don't speak to a public audience the same way you would to a university audience. Even when your listeners are educated, professional people, it's often the case that they have been out of school for so long and have spent so much of their energies in practical work that their conceptual apparatus has become a little rusty, making abstract, theoretical discourse a challenge for them.

I've had this experience with physicians. I'd just finished my presentation as speaker at an annual banquet of a local physician's guild. The thrust of my talk was that the dignity of the physician's vocation was bound up with the power over life and death. The power to save is at once the power to kill. But when the physician elects to kill people, as in the performance of abortions and euthanasia, he or she subverts the medical ethos and returns it to that of the medicine man of old — the most feared person in the village since everyone knew that he would kill or heal, depending on what you paid him to do. I certainly didn't regard it as a particularly abstract or difficult presentation to follow. In fact, I had the impression that the audience seemed to be enjoying it as I went along and when I'd finished they gave me an enthusiastic applause. But a few minutes later, the host of the banquet, who was sitting at my right, said to me: "This kind of talk is good for us to hear; we don't get the chance very often to think about abstract, philosophical issues." This, from a neurosurgeon; the man was obviously no dunce!

Regarding the choice of words and overall delivery, my experience has been that it is best to use common, everyday words, preferably words that are concrete and have strong imagery. In my early days of public speaking on abortion, a sociology teacher gave me very good advice after hearing me over the radio. Politely but firmly she said to me: "When you use expressions like "*a fortiori*," do you assume your listeners know what they mean?" I was so accustomed to using that term in the ivied halls of the university that I'd come to treat it as part of ordinary language. Although it might be considered ordinary in the academic world, it surely is not so in the outside world. Thereafter, I abandoned the use of that expression along with any others that would strike the ear of the public as obscure, exotic or daunting. On the radio interview in question, I'd apparently said something like this: "If killing an innocent human being is wrong, then, *a fortiori*, deliberately killing an unborn child is wrong." Thereafter, I said: "If killing an innocent human being is wrong, then it follows that deliberately killing an unborn child is wrong."

Short sentences are better than long ones. I was amazed on reading John Henry Newman's *The Idea of a University* to learn that the book was really a series of lectures he delivered at the founding of the University of Dublin. Its sentences are long and often full of qualifying clauses. How could the audiences follow him through all that? The fact is that before the age of electronic information and entertainment, people were used to words: they listened, they wrote, they read. They could follow long, involved discussions, such as the reportedly sometimes eight hours long Lincoln-Douglas debates. In contrast, we children of today's video culture are accustomed to getting our news of the world by sound-bytes; consequently, we have shorter attention spans and are less adept at the use of language. When preparing your public presentation, what you write down may look good on paper, but its oral impact is another matter. For example, I've found the following effective. When referred to in public as "pro-life," I immediately respond: "I'm not pro-life, I'm anti-abortion." The power of this retort is that it is short, clear, and emphatic. This gets my audience's attention and lets them know that the reason I'm standing before them is to talk about the special evil of killing the unborn.

A couple of debates taught me the importance of spelling things out. By neglecting to make explicit a step or two in my argument, I enabled my opponents to turn the argument to their advantage. In response to my opponent's claim that women will continue to have abortions whether legal or not, I observed that people continue to commit rape and car theft – in fact, the number of these crimes is on the rise, but nobody would suppose that we'd better abolish the laws prohibiting them since people are going to do them anyway. My opponent, a sharp graduate of Yale Law School, quickly responded: "We're talking about a woman's Constitutional right to reproductive freedom and he [me] is identifying women who choose to exercise that right with rapists and car thieves."

Until that moment, it never occurred to me that I was assuming that there was no need to explicate all the steps of the argument; they seemed so obvious. But the question is, "obvious to whom?" "To me?" The problem is that I use them all the time and repetition creates efficiency and efficiency demands economy of means; in other words, shorthand. Fine for me, but not for the audience.

From that day forward, I made sure to lay out all the steps of my argument. No more shorthand if I could help it. I now take the trouble to put the matter thus: If the rationale for repealing a law is simply that large numbers of people refuse to obey it, that implies that *any* widely disobeyed law should be repealed. But no sane person would buy that. True, we sometimes repeal laws that society refuses to obey, such as Prohibition, but there is more to it than that. The decision to repeal Prohibition was also based on the fact that, in moderation, the consumption of alcoholic beverages is not harmful. Suppose infanticide were widely practiced, even though against the law. Imagine repealing that law for that reason!

If induced abortion is, as I argue, the deliberate killing of an innocent human being, that is a serious enough reason for making (keeping) it illegal and enforcing the law. The FBI reported that last year almost one million automobiles were stolen nationwide. Why don't we say therefore that auto theft should be legalized since large numbers of people insist on stealing automobiles even though it's against the law? The answer is that we regard auto theft as a serious violation of the right to property. The fact that many people choose to flout the law doesn't mitigate the seriousness of the threat that auto theft poses to society. When the civil rights laws were passed in the 1960s, many segregationists publicly announced their resolve to disobey them. Did society thereby decide the laws were a bad idea because many people, including a couple of governors and many legislators in the south, promised to continue segregation in public schools, diners, buses? They did not. When Governor Orval Faubus of Arkansas said he would personally block the entrance to a public school in Little Rock to prevent a little black girl from entering, President Eisenhower sent in troops from the airborne to ensure her safe entrance to the school.

Clearly, no act can be justified, legally or morally, solely by appealing to the fact that people are going to do it whether legal or not. When you hear someone arguing that way for the legalization of abortion, it's a safe bet they're ducking the crucial question, "Is induced abortion the deliberate killing of an innocent human being?"

I suspect it's just because pro-abortion advocates have such a hard time handling that question that they're constantly on the alert to pounce on any statement their opponents make that promises to whisk the discussion as far from it as possible. Shorthand arguments like the one above offer them an engraved invitation to do it. I took the same kind of hit, but thankfully with much less damage, on another occasion when using a couple of examples that seemed to me clear and unambiguous illustrations of my argument that induced abortion betrays, at the least, a willingness to kill an innocent human being.

The first example was of a hunter who fired his rifle into a clump of bushes on the assumption that its rustling branches indicated the presence of a deer, but to his horror he found that he'd killed another hunter. I pointed out that the court would hold him liable for his deed on the premise that he was wrong to shoot his rifle without first making sure of his target. I went on to say that, in light of all the evidence from embryology and common sense – a human father and a human mother produce the fetus; if it's not a human being, what is it? —, it would be unreasonable to deny that the fetus is a human being. Even if one took the more moderate stance that it *might not* be a human being – and this would be quite a stretch —, how does deliberately aborting it morally differ from deliberately firing into bushes when one is not sure if the target is human or animal?

The second example comes under the rubric, "We do not play light with the things we prize." Imagine a hiker who stumbles upon a canvass bag with the words stamped across its side, "Acme Armored Car Service." He cannot open it because the zipper is fastened with a heavy lock for which he obviously has no key. Kneading the bag with his hands, he draws the conclusion that it contains thick bundles of paper about the size of paper money. He could carry the bag back to his cabin where he has the tools to open it or, better yet, inform the armored car company of its existence. Instead he decides it's too much trouble to carry the bag and leaves it there without any thought of returning to reclaim it. We could infer from the hiker's behavior that he places little value on money. Of course, he can't be sure there's money inside; but given that it feels like it and it's an armored car company's bag, the probability that it is money is better than even. If he cared about money, he'd want to find out or inform the company.

Equally, the legalization of elective abortion proclaims society's indifference to human life. Otherwise, the people would at least say, "Wait a minute! Let's be careful about allowing elective or indeed any form of induced abortion. We might be killing human beings."

In reply, my opponent said, "We're talking about women's reproductive rights and lives here, not about deer and money bags." How many points did her grandstanding score with the audience? I don't know, but I realized that it wouldn't hurt to bulletproof the examples; they were, after all, good ones. What I did from then on was to introduce them with the qualification: "Of course abortion and hunting are different kinds of actions." I would then emphasize a point upon which all reasonable people would agree, to wit, that no matter what the category of action, if you're about to do a life-threatening act, the morally responsible thing is first to find out if the intended victim is a human being. If we demand that the hunter take reasonable steps to ensure that he is not firing upon another human being, then does it not follow that we must demand that we embark upon a reasonable exploration of the available evidence on the status of the fetus before legalizing induced abortion?"

One last comment under this heading: watch your logic. We all want to go into a debate armed with the most logical and trenchant arguments possible. That, of course, makes good sense. Nevertheless, it helps to put a human face on your logic. If big words and abstract ideas can intimidate listeners, you can count on logic having the same effect. Brandishing your logical skills as you would a weapon risks spoiling a good presentation by creating defensive reactions among your listeners. I discovered this point during my early years on the debate stump:

> May 31, 1973
>
> Dear…,
>
> This is to acknowledge the appearance of Mr. Ray Dennehy before two of my Family Life classes on April 26, 1973. His purpose was to present the "anti" side of the abortion question and the format placed him in a session with a speaker representing the pro side.
>
> He did a great job. His command of the historical nature of the position of the Catholic church(*sic*) and several classical philosophers was excellent. Some students felt personally (*sic*) attacked when he called upon his experience and training in logic. He did not use this as an attack of course, but the effect was there.
>
> On the whole, he did a fine job of representing an unpopular position – unpopular with the majority of students.
>
> I will definitely use him as a speaker on this issue in the future.
>
> Thank you for your help.
>
> Sincerely,
>
> [Signed]
>
> Henry M. Gunn Senior High School
>
> Palo Alto Unified School District

WAVING RED FLAGS

Sales representatives, politicians, and the mavens of advertising are hyper-sensitive to the dangers of saying things that are likely to annoy their audience unnecessarily. That sensitivity is especially important when debating a topic as emotionally charged as abortion. Sometimes, the audience is hostile toward you before you utter a word just because they know you're against abortion; they're waiting for an excuse to pounce on you. At other times it's not the general audience but various people in it who've come in with a chip on their shoulders, but there's no point in needlessly intensifying their antagonism toward you either. Here are three examples of what not to say.

I was debating an ACLU attorney at the University of California's Hastings School of Law in San Francisco. One of the panelists asked me how I would deal with the religions in which abortion was permitted. "Doesn't your position against the legalization of abortion collide," he asked, "with the freedom of religion?" I gave what seemed to me at the time a cogent and facile reply: "Like the Hebrew National Sausage Company, even a liberal democracy such as ours must in such cases appeal to a higher authority." My reply was met with groans and other inarticulate sounds of disapproval among the audience. I assumed that everyone was familiar with the television commercial in which a Jehovah-like bass voice justified the claim that Hebrew National brand sausages were pure beef, even though the Federal government allows additives, by saying, "We appeal to a higher authority," at which moment a picture of Mount Sinai *a la* Cecil B. DeMille appeared with the sight and sound of thunder and lightening above it. Unfortunately, many members of the audience were unfamiliar with it and interpreted my words as anti-Semitic. My gaffe.

On another occasion, one of my students and I were debating two members of Planned Parenthood at U.C., Berkeley. She was doing a first-rate job, especially considering that this was her first debate and that she was doing it before 700 students at a school famous for its liberal views. She retained her composure throughout and spoke in an unassuming but cogent manner. We were now well into the second hour of the debate when a member of the audience asked her how she reconciled the pro-life stance with the ambush murder of a physician in Florida by an anti-abortionist. She answered that it was a kind of poetic justice. In *Roe v. Wade* the State had given the right to kill to ordinary citizens and the ambusher was only exercising this newly attained right. I think her statement was correct, but I don't think she should have said it, at least not in that bald fashion. It came across as smug and insensitive, even though she was neither. As I recall, some members of the audience thought it humorous (maybe darkly so) while others expressed sounds of disapproval. The questioner, however, said: "Whatever respect I had for you up till now has been lost because of that answer." He was, I agree, pompous, self-righteous, and clearly guilty of making an *ad hominem* response. But her answer gave him the opportunity to say things that at least offered the other members of the audience the image of an anti-abortionist who was smug and insensitive. And as I noted earlier, the irreducible fact is that audiences, even sophisticated university audiences, are impressionistic.

Although I've already cited the following example under another heading, it applies under the present heading as well. In another U.C. Berkeley debate, my partner was in charge of education for her statewide pro-life group. She announced at the beginning of the event that she'd had an abortion a few years back, but has since reached the conclusion that what she did was wrong. The fact that she'd "been there, done that" probably created a plus for our side among the women in the audience; at least no one could accuse her of naiveté. When asked what she thought of abortion for women who got pregnant by rape, she asked the questioner, "Do you mean 'true rape?'" The audience, certainly its female representation, was not pleased with the question. I think I know what she had in mind by implying the distinction, but, in any case, it is a distinction that is best left unspoken under those circumstances. The atmosphere on many campuses was then, as now, thick with complaints by women of "date rape," and the suggestion that any of these women were not really raped, whatever the reasons given for it, is sure to turn large numbers of the females in the audience against the speaker who uttered it.

AS IN POLITICS, SO AT THE PODIUM: PERCEPTION *IS* REALITY

The importance of the impression you convey to your audience cannot be too heavily stressed. I have to say it again, audiences are impressionistic. They form their opinion of you, positive or negative, on your appearance, your overall manner and other things, many of which have nothing to do with the content of your presentation. The experts in advertising and public image-making are acutely aware of such matters: the color and cut of your clothes, hair style, general facial expression, tone of voice; all these and more they treat with the greatest importance. A survey in the aftermath of the famous Nixon-Kennedy presidential debates gave powerful testimony to this truth. Among the people surveyed, the majority of those who watched the debates on television thought that Kennedy won them, while among those who listened to them over the radio, the majority thought that Nixon won. Kennedy looked young; he exuded idealism and vitality; he sounded intelligent and sincere. Nixon looked older; and not only was he not good looking, his manner and facial expressions conveyed the impression of craftiness, even dishonesty. A series of five presidential television debates was won and lost on the basis of impressions.

My wife chooses my wardrobe for a debate: suit, shirt, and tie. Apparently pinstriped suits are bad for such occasions because they convey the sense of elitism. Too bad, they're my favorites. And a red tie? Forget it; I understand that it intimidates the audience with its statement of power. Recently, I've been appearing for my debates with no coat and sporting judiciously chosen shirt, tie and suspenders. I think it's the right choice . It conveys the impression of the working, no nonsense professor.

If I'm going to have a debate partner, I prefer a woman with the following profile: young, attractive, articulate and conspicuously intelligent; preferably an attorney, physician, nurse, professor, executive type. A woman on the stage dispels the image of the anti-abortion movement as run by males and worse by "oppressor males." A woman who is young and attractive gets positive attention from the young women in the audience; they can see that she, too, must be under the same sexual pressure as they and so she might be worth listening to. They look over at me and see a grandfather. "What does he know about life in today's world?" True, from all reports, the young in my audiences are impressed with what I say, even if they end up still enshrouded in their pro–abortion haze. Still. there's no substitute for the power of one's peers. And a woman who is either professional or bound for the professions connects with the aspirations of the college audience. A woman who is conspicuously intelligent and articulate shows that she's no Barbie Doll; she is someone worth listening to.

Impressions should not matter. In a perfect world, it would be what the speaker said that counted, regardless of age, gender, looks, and walk of life. But this is no perfect world. If it were, we wouldn't be standing on a stage debating whether we have the right to destroy innocent, unborn human beings.

CHAPTER SIX

RESCUING THE HIDDEN CHILD

"If I were to be taken for a fool by knights, grandees, the noble of spirit and the high-born, I would consider it an irreparable affront; but that I should be thought crazy by scholars who have never entered upon or even touched the pathways of chivalry: for this I don't give two hoots. A knight am I and a knight I shall die, if it please the Most High."

The Adventures of Don Quixote, Pt. II, Ch. XXXII

It's a safe bet that over 99.9% of those who are against abortion believe that the fetus is a human being. So it is understandable that, when they want to argue their position, they should start off by trying to prove that the fetus is a human being from the moment of conception. That's exactly what I tried to do back in the 1960s when I first got into the abortion debate. But my thinking always ran into the same stone wall. Being in the Aristotelian–Thomistic philosophical tradition, I held, as I still do, that it is impossible to explain distinctive human operations, like knowing and choosing, without positing an immaterial soul. Because it is impossible for contraries to produce each other – you can't get apples from oranges —, it was clear that the soul did not arise from our material being, for the material can't produce the immaterial. But that meant that some outside agent, God, must imbue each of his human creations with an immaterial soul.

Did he do this at the moment of conception or later on in gestation? Since it is, at least, possible that God could choose to imbue an immaterial soul into the conceptus later rather than sooner and since it is impossible for us to know the mind and will of God on such matters, the validity of that question must be acknowledged. Were Aristotle and Thomas Aquinas correct in holding that human ensoulment occurs later in gestation? As long as I couldn't put that possibility to bed, how could I argue that the unborn is a human being from the moment of conception?

Don't misunderstand me. Thomas Aquinas accepted the Aristotelian biology, which assumed an economy of nature: nature never uses a higher form of life to do what a lower form can do. Since the budding of male genitalia is first visible by the naked eye at forty days, he agreed with Aristotle that the male got his soul at that time; and since the budding of female genitalia is first visible at eighty days, that the female got her soul then.

Granted, all that represents the biology of the ancient world and is a far cry from contemporary biology. Thomas Aquinas died in 1274. The male sperm was discovered in 1677 by Hamm, thanks to the development of the microscope; and in the 19th century the female ovum was identified. In 1827, Karl Ernst von Boar advanced the idea that both male and female contribute to the production of human life by a process called "conception." With the subsequent discovery of DNA and, thanks to Watson and Crick, the discovery of how it works, it is now clear that from the moment of conception no constituent addition is made; the conceptus simply unfolds, according to the "blueprint" of the DNA code, in what is known as a morphological process. But you needn't subscribe to the ancient biology to be unsure when the moment of human life begins. To say that nothing is added is to say that nothing *material* is added. The principle that contraries cannot be derived from each other still holds. If the human soul is immaterial, then God must create it in the unborn at some given moment. That could be immediately at conception or at some later moment. Who can say for sure?

Although I was, and am, 99.9999% certain that the unborn is human from the very beginning of its existence, the thing in a debate is to produce the most powerful argument you can to support your position, and that means, among other things, avoiding assumptions and weak premises. In my case, the position was that direct abortion is morally unjustifiable, socially destructive, and lethal to democracy. In the first chapter, I said that in time I was able to forge into a powerful debating weapon the claim I made in my first radio appearance, namely, that we were proceeding with legalized abortion on request without determining whether the fetus to be aborted is a human being. It didn't take me long to come to the conclusion that my argument on the debate stump would be more powerful if I abandoned the attempt to demonstrate that the fetus was a human being from the moment of conception and argued instead from a premise of probability. Over the years it has proven to be very effective.

Some may find my argument thin because it doesn't really come to grips with the relevant philosophical issues. My answer is that there is a huge difference between a presentation suitable for an academic or otherwise learned audience and one suitable for debate before a large audience whose members have varied intellectual and cultural backgrounds. For example, as I noted previously, when lecturing on abortion in my bioethics course, I have the time, as many days as I wish, to address the arguments of gradualists, such as Mary Ann Warren and Michael Tooley, who argue that the fetus develops into a person, an event that does not occur until some months after birth. My course gives me the chronological wherewithal to delve into the history of the word "person" — its philosophical, theological, and legal uses – to show how these writers base their distinction on the assumption of the correctness of Descartes' definition of man as "a thinking substance" in contrast to the classical view — Aristotle, Boethius, Thomas Aquinas – which holds that rationality is not our essence or defining characteristic of our human nature but the most important power of our souls. I also have the leisure to address arguments like that advanced by Judith Jarvis Thomson: the justification for induced abortion does not depend on whether or not the fetus is a human being or a person but rather on the principle that a woman has no obligation to keep a being inside her if she does not wish it.

In my debates, I'm ready to get into these kinds of issues should the occasion present itself during the questions and comments from the audience. But, as I pointed out in Chapter 5, the debate format allows you only a little time to present your case, so you've got to settle for a lean argument. Yes, the argument is thin, but the thinner it is, the sharper its cutting edge. Under those circumstances, your aim should be to leave your audience with one or two crucial ideas clearly etched in their minds.

I confess that the one question I've always dreaded, but remarkably have never had to face in my debates, is that of twinning. Some argue that the phenomenon of monozygotic twinning shows that the embryo is not a person until at least implantation, after which point twinning no longer occurs. The reason they give? Because in identical twining one embryo splits into two embryos, the original one cannot be a human person. I've consulted a noted embryologist on this point and went away with the impression that the phenomenon of human twinning is poorly understood, even by those in the field. I do not find the objection from twinning at all conclusive. Because twinning only occurs in some conceptions, the claim that the zygote can't therefore be a single individual substance loses its strength. But the phenomenon of twinning disturbs me nevertheless because I can't explain how one human being can become two.

For my debates, on the other hand, I've honed an argument designed to be clean, cogent and quick, aiming to rivet the audience's attention on one point: "Is induced abortion the direct killing of an innocent person?" Hopefully, they will never think the same way about abortion again. And I've reason to believe this approach has been successful. Occasionally, the directors of the program at the University of California, Berkeley forward comments and letters written to me by students present at the debate. One comment appears regularly: "This is the first time I've heard a rational argument against abortion." Even those letters critical of my argument often betray an inner turmoil, signaled by their flimsy objections, usually cliché ridden, such as, "If you can't trust me with a choice, how can you trust me with a child?"

Here's how I proceed.

THE ARGUMENT

If the fetus is not a human being, then no reasons need be offered to justify abortion. All that society could legally require of a woman who wishes an abortion is what the United States Supreme Court (*Roe v. Wade*, 1973) stipulated: (1) that the procedure be performed by licensed personnel; (2) that it be performed on accredited premises, to wit, a hospital or clinic.

But if the fetus *is* a human being, then induced abortion is the direct killing of an innocent human being, and what reason could justify that? What could justify the more than one million legal abortions performed yearly in this country? If the fetus is a human being, then induced abortion not only violates the right to life but strikes at the very heart of democracy. According to the Declaration of Independence, the rights of life, liberty, and the pursuit of happiness are conferred by nature and its Creator, not by governments. Of all rights, the right to life is primary. Of course the others, like freedom of speech, peaceable public assembly and worship, are crucial. But the right to life is primary in the sense that all other rights presuppose it. A government that failed to protect that right could not, in the name of consistency, be faulted for failing to protect the other rights. I would go further and say that the right to life extends beyond the political and social. Life is, after all, the biological presupposition of individual and collective striving. If I am not allowed to live and grow, if I simply don't exist, then I can be neither virtuous nor evil, neither a success nor a failure.

Abortion is killing, for it is feticide, the destruction of a living fetus. Strictly speaking, "abortion" is the expulsion of a pre-viable fetus; but craniotomy and embryotomy are also commonly classified as abortions.

Clearly, a lot rides on our answer to the question, "Is the fetus, which induced abortion kills, a human being?" How do we go about settling it?

First, the fetus is the product of a human father and a human mother. If it's not a human being, what is it?

Second, so far as I can make out, the scientific evidence comes down on the side of the fetus being a human being. Consider the following examples:

> Essentially all higher animals start their lives from a single cell, the fertilized *ovum* (*zygote*). As its name implies, the zygote has a dual origin from two gametes — a spermatozoon from the male parent and an ovum from the female parent. The time of fertilization, when the spermatozoon meets the egg, represents the starting point in the life history, or *ontogeny*, of the individual. In its broadest sense, ontogeny refers to the individual's entire life span. (Bruce M. Carlson, *Patten's Foundations of Embryology*

> Fertilization in mammals normally represents the beginning of life for a new individual. (R. Yanagimachi, "Mammalian Fertilization," *The Physiology of Reproduction*, E. Krobil, J. Neill, *et al.* ed.

> Fertilization is an important landmark because, under ordinary circumstances, a new, genetically distinct human organism is thereby formed. (R. O'Rahilly, "One Hundred Years of Human Embryology," *Issues and Reviews in Teratology*

Third, the field of medicine that concerns itself with both the unborn and the mother, known as perinatology, also affirms the fetus as an individual human life, but, as we might expect, from the standpoint of a patient:

> Since World War II...the status of the fetus has been elevated to that of a patient who should be given the same meticulous care by the physician that we have long given the pregnant woman."

> *(Williams Obstetrics,* 17th ed. [1985], p. 139)

Fourth, as late as 1963, Planned Parenthood did not hesitate to echo its acceptance of this view of the human fetus. In its official pamphlet for that year, we find the following:

> Is birth control an abortion?" Definitely not. An abortion kills the life of a baby after it has begun...Birth control merely postpones the beginning of life.

> *Planned Parenthood* pamphlet, August, 1963

Fifth, In *People v. Davis,* 1993, the California State Supreme Court ruled that a third party who kills a fetus could be charged with murder, even though the fetus is nonviable. The court hastened to add that this ruling does not nullify a woman's Constitutional right to an abortion.

The legal schizophrenia in this ruling fascinates. True, the court here recognizes two categories of murder, homicide and feticide. But "murder" is by definition homicide: "unjustifiable homicide." If it means anything to rule that a third party who kills a fetus may be charged with murder, it is because the fetus is a human being: feticide is homicide. Intriguing, no? The being that a woman may legally kill in the name of her Constitutional right to privacy is the very same being that is "murdered" if killed by a third party. Behind this semantic madness lies an uneasiness over the status of the victim of abortion.

Sixth, there is a logical difficulty in denying that the fetus is a human being from the moment of conception. Mammalian reproduction does not produce a different species or a subspecies of its own which then develops into its own species. Specifically, a rabbit embryo is a rabbit; a polliwog is a frog, etc. From conception every constituent element is present in the DNA; it's all there from the start. But if nothing is added, then how does the fetus become a human being? If it's not a human being at time-1, how is it that it is a human being at time-2? Of course, if one wished to bring God into the discussion, one could then argue that the fetus is not a human being at time-1 but becomes one at time-2 when God imbues it with an immaterial soul. But that's a move that most pro-abortionists are unwilling to make. Absent any appeal to divine intervention, the challenge remains: "If the fetus is not a human being (or person) at time-1, how can it become one at time-2?"

In a brilliant article, "Personhood and the Conception Event," Robert Joyce employs the distinction between a mechanistic model and an organic model to cinch this point. Imagine all the components of a watch scattered on a table; next imagine someone assembling them into a watch. At time-1, there is no watch; at time-2, when all the parts are in place, there is a watch. In this example of a mechanism, a thing can become what it is not because an external agent so organizes it. The agent could have organized the parts differently so that rather than a watch the result was a sculpture or some kind of Rube Goldberg contraption. But in the case of an organism, there is no assignable external agent assembling its components to become something at time-2 that it is not at time-1. The organism simply unfolds according to its DNA blueprint, explicating what it already is.

When the pro-abortion movement started, people stopped talking about "unborn babies" in favor of "fetuses." The purpose of this semantic switch was, if not to redefine the unborn out of the human race, at least verbally to shield us from abortion's horrible reality. It's an old story: we kill with words before we kill with deeds. In a previous chapter, I observed that the news media use both terms, "fetus" or "unborn baby," depending on the story. This is not surprising, given its commitment to the principle, "Dog Bites Man!" is not news; "Man Bites Dog!" That's news. When they are reporting on abortion, the media use "fetus"; but when reporting a life-saving intrauterine surgery, then it becomes an "unborn baby." The reference to a baby makes it a human-interest story. Besides, they obviously wouldn't want to talk about saving fetuses when they're the things it's a woman's Constitutional right to terminate. Recite the following aloud a few times: "When we kill it, it's a fetus; when we save it, it's a baby."

But the wishes of pro-abortionists notwithstanding, "fetus" does not mean "subhuman." It simply indicates a stage of development. There are dog fetuses and horse fetuses, just as there are dog adolescents and horse adolescents and dog adults and horse adults. Similarly, there are human fetuses, human infants, human adolescents and human adults. So?

What about the objection that the above is a purely materialistic representation of what it is to be a human being when, in truth, a fully fledged human being is not present in the womb until God imbues it with an immaterial soul? As mentioned earlier, the answer to this is that there is no way of telling when that happens; it might have an immaterial soul from the moment of conception. It would thus be impossible to know whether an early stage induced abortion killed a human being. I'll come back to this point shortly.

What we know from the available evidence is that from the moment of conception, we have an individual being with forty-six chromosomes and that that being is genetically unique, which means that it is not part of the woman's body; for every cell in her body has the same genetic structure, which is different from that of the conceptus. By twenty-one days, the fetus has its own beating heart and its own blood type; by eight weeks, it has its own brain, capable of producing brain waves; by ten to twelve weeks all organs are in place.

In light of all the above evidence, it's rationally indefensible to deny that the fetus is a human being. There is far more evidence in favor of its being human than against it. The only reasonable objection to those who hold that the fetus is a human being is that that position cannot be certain but must instead be a matter of probability. If it is reasonable to suppose that the fetus *probably* is a human being, then one could come back with the objection that by the very meaning of "probable," it must then be reasonable to suppose that the fetus *probably* is not a human being.

Thus, a minimalist interpretation of the evidence leads us to this premise: whether the fetus is a human being is a matter of probability. But this means that the justification of induced abortion when there is doubt about its being human is the willingness to kill a human being. Consider, for example, the case of the hunter who fires his rifle into a clump of rustling bushes in the belief that a deer is there. When he gets to the bushes to claim his quarry, he finds to his horror that he has killed another hunter. Both morally and legally he has acted unjustifiably. The court would rule that he should not have fired when he couldn't be sure of his target, especially during hunting season when it was likely that other hunters would be in the area. Now if the odds that it was another human being rather than a deer were one hundred thousand to one, the district attorney probably would not hold him liable for the shooting. But what if the odds were one in ten? One in five? What are the odds that the fetus, produced by a human father and a human mother, is a human being?

We do not play light with the things we prize. Suppose a hiker in the wilderness came across a canvass bag with a heavy lock on its zipper opening. On its front in huge letters are the words, "Acme Armored Car Service." From the feel of the bag's contents, the hiker has the impression that it contains paper money. It could be something else, canceled checks, perhaps, but that would be unlikely since canceled checks are hardly objects coveted by thieves. Could it be personnel records, newspaper clippings, or the like? Possible but less probable than the suspicion that the bag contains paper money. But how is he going to settle the matter? Since he doesn't have at hand the tools needed to open the bag, he will have to carry it back to town. Suppose, however, he decides that that requires more effort than he is willing to expend and he leaves the bag lying where he found it. We could infer from the hiker's behavior that he valued his convenience more than money. Equally, to justify induced abortion while acknowledging that it may be an innocent human being that one is killing is to imply that innocent human beings, at least those in the womb, anyway, are less important than the reasons for which one gets induced abortions.

I submit to you that even on a minimalist interpretation of the evidence, induced abortion is morally unjustifiable; for it bespeaks at least a willingness to kill an innocent human being, a willingness to make human life a negotiable item; and what is that but a willingness therefore to repudiate an indispensable component of our democratic charter — the right to life?

This inference exposes the bankruptcy of the pro-choice position. No society is pro-choice in an absolute sense. Our democratic society recognizes and protects my right to say in public that the books in your home library are tawdry, salacious, and harmful to morals. But it will not allow me to invade your home and destroy your books. My freedom of conscience and thought – the right to believe and think what I wish – doesn't allow me to trample your right to own such books as you wish. Again, society acknowledges my freedom of religion, my right to worship as I please. But that right isn't absolute. Society will not acknowledge my right to sacrifice a young virgin on my altar, no matter how fervently convinced I am that that is the only form of sacrifice pleasing to God. Here my exercise of religion collides with someone else's right to life.

Equally, since the right to life extends to all, it follows that no one, not even the mother, ought to have the right to kill an unborn child. You could argue that a sane adult should have the right to embroider his or her skin with a tattoo, be sterilized, or undergo cosmetic surgery because such acts affect only his or her own body. But the fetus is not part of the woman's body. What organ, muscle or skeletal part has limbs, organs, its own blood type, and unique genetic structure? One searches in vain through *Gray's Anatomy* for a body part called "fetus."

What Abraham Lincoln said in debate with Douglas about the slavery question applies perfectly to today's pro-choice position:

> [W]hen Judge Douglas says he "don't care whether slavery is voted up or down,"...he cannot thus argue logically if he sees anything wrong in it.... He cannot say that he would as soon see a wrong voted up as voted down. When Judge Douglas says that whoever, or whatever community, wants slaves, they have a right to have them, he is perfectly logical if there is nothing wrong in the institution; but if you admit that it is wrong, he can-

not logically say that anybody has a right to do a wrong.

What justification is there for making abortion a matter of choice? I've argued that even if one does not go so far as to say that the fetus is a human being, the available evidence – the continuity of mammalian development, the distinctively human chromosomal identity from the moment of conception, the fact that nothing constitutive is added throughout gestation – makes it strongly probable that it is a human being and hence that induced abortion bespeaks a willingness to kill an innocent human being. That is clearly immoral and, to quote Lincoln, nobody has a right to do a wrong. The choice to undergo an abortion is not a freedom that a democratic and, indeed, a civilized society can permit.

CLARIFICATIONS

After I present my argument, the format of the debate usually allows me to amplify fundamental points. The opportunity may present itself in the rebuttal to my opponent's argument or in response to the audience's questions and comments. For example, now and then someone in the audience will ask me if my argument for the humanity of the fetus does not attribute more validity to the claims of science than can be justified. To this I typically reply:

First, I'm not assuming that any scientific consensus is the last word on any topic of scientific inquiry. I'm quite aware of the contingency of any empirical claim as well as of the controversies that continue to swirl around the claims to realism of scientific statements, particularly as they pertain to putative submicroscopic entities. My reason for turning to the biological sciences is that they are the appropriate disciplines to consult in order to discover what answers the scientific community gives to key questions: "When is the being produced by the union of sperm and egg alive?" "When is it human?" "When is it a human life?"

My second qualification is to distinguish between utterances a scientist makes that are *legitimately scientific* and those that, although uttered by a scientist in a scientific context, are not scientific at all but are instead philosophical, political, or subjective. For example, biologist, Leon Rosenberg, of Yale University, told a U.S. Senate hearing in 1981 that he knew of no scientific evidence showing when human life begins. But I do not think that he used the word "scientific" here in the sense in which it is applied to biology or embryology. This seems clear from the reason he gave for his disclaimer, to wit, "the complex quality of humanness." "Humanness" is not the way a scientist talks when he wishes to offer scientifically rigorous utterances. The term is, on the contrary, vague and, if not used in a philosophical or theological definition — in which case it surely wouldn't be scientific, as in humanness as the essence of man, it's smudgy. Earlier in this chapter, I quoted from O'Rahilly as one of three examples to support my claim that the mainstream position of embryologists is that, from conception, we have a human being. I now present the statement again, but in the context of the sentence that precedes it and the one that follows it in order to show how the two qualifications — scientifically legitimate and scientifically illegitimate utterances by scientists — come together:

> The status of the early human embryo is an evaluative rather than a directly scientific question. Fertilization is an important landmark because, under ordinary circumstances, a new, genetically distinct human organism is thereby formed. Opinions are divided, however, on the philosophical conclusion as to whether the human organism is a human person from fertilization or only from some later time.

Notice the juxtaposition of terms, "human embryo" and "human organism," on the one hand, and "human person," on the other. The first two terms are scientific, while the third is, as O'Rahilly notes, philosophical (as well as theological and legal). Now my point in citing these texts is to show that when embryologists speak scientifically about the status of the fetus, they say it is a human being or human individual. That is probably why when O'Rahilly says above, "The status of the early human embryo is an evaluative rather than scientific question," he uses the term "human person." Apparently, what is evaluative about the status of the embryo is not whether it is a human being but whether it is a person. I'll address the philosophical debate over the *personhood* of the fetus below.

MORE CLARIFICATIONS

Personhood vs. the "Merely Human"

What is presented here is not the "clean, quick and cogent" form of argument I use in debates but an amplification of the points I try to make on those occasions. If the opportunity to amplify presents itself during the question and answer segment of the debate, this is how I proceed. I almost always use Mary Ann Warren's "The Moral and Legal Status of Abortion," though sometimes I've used Michael Tooley's, book, *Abortion and Infanticide*. But I prefer to use Warren not only because it created quite a stir in academic circles when it first appeared in *The Monist* in 1973 but, more so, because it's perhaps the best known of the "developmentalist" pro-abortion arguments.

Warren argues that a fetus has "genetic humanity" (is a human being) but not "moral humanity" (is not a person). She regards five traits as central to the concept of person:

1. consciousness (of objects and events external and/or internal to the being), and in particular the capacity to feel pain;

2. reasoning (the *developed* capacity to solve new and relatively complex problems);

3. self-motivated activity (activity which is relatively independent of either genetic or direct external control);

4. the capacity to communicate, by whatever means, messages of an indefinite variety of types, that is, not just with an indefinite number of possible contents, but on indefinitely many possible topics;

5. the presence of self-concepts, and self-awareness, either individual or racial, or both.

Warren speculates that (1) and (2) alone might be sufficient conditions for personhood and more probably (1)-(3) are sufficient. No one of the five may be necessary in order to be a person, though (1)-(3) seems to be necessary conditions for it. At all events, she insists that no being which satisfies none of the five criteria is a person.

Warren then proceeds to argue that because the fetus is not now a person but will develop into one, it is a *potential* person. The mother is an actual person. Because the rights of an actual person override the rights of a merely potential person, it follows that the mother can abort the fetus without violating its right to life and without committing murder.

MY REPLY

One way of justifying the deliberate killing of members of a special class is to argue that they are not human beings; but that cannot be done in the case of the fetus, for it is a *human* fetus. The only remaining way to disenfranchise it then is to exclude it from the community of persons. This is the same gambit employed by the U.S. Supreme Court in the last century in the *Dred Scot* decision. Blacks, Justice Taney ruled, were only three-fifths persons under the Constitution and may thus be used as chattel property.

The concept of person is broader than the concept of human being. You can conceive of beings that are persons but not human beings, e.g., God, angels, extra-terrestrials, in short, any rational being that is not a member of homo sapiens. But what does it mean to say that you can have a human being that is not a person? The concept of a rectangle is broader than the concept of a square. But we don't infer from this that a square is therefore not a rectangle.

Pro-abortionists like Warren think they can make such an inference because they are functionalists. The fetus does not function in a certain way; it is not, for example, self-aware; therefore it is not a person. The functionalist argument fails to distinguish between rationality or self-awareness as a power of man's essence and the exercise of that power. Truly, the mature human is able to exercise his rational powers while the fetus cannot. But the fetus is still a human being and a person, for like the developed human being, it possesses the essence man. It is not the exercise of reason and volition– what may be called "secondary act" – that makes a human being a person but rather the exercise of the act of existence peculiar to man's essence, what may be called "primary act." The exercise of reason and volition, along with the other higher operations, is admittedly the fulfillment of these powers, but that is just my point: Their exercise does not make a being a person but instead fulfills his or her essence. Their exercise indicates that the being so acting is a person but it surely does not make him or her a person. Rather it is being a person that allows a being to act according to reason and choice.

Warren's functionalist criteria for personhood presuppose the validity of the Cartesian conception of man. Descartes defined man as "a being that thinks," rejecting Aristotle's conception of "rational animal" on the ground that it fell short of the criteria of the "clear and the distinct" for acceptable ideas. Now there is an enormous difference between saying that the essence of the human person is rational activity or self-awareness, on the one hand, and rational animality, on the other. In the latter case, rationality is a power of the rational soul, not its essence. I say that experience shows that Descartes is wrong and Aristotle is right. The superiority of rational animal is that it defines man in terms of his essence or nature, not in terms of powers that properly belong to that essence. Because man is a rational animal, he has the natural potential to know; but until that potential is actualized in particular acts of knowing, it remains in a state of potency. Yet it would be absurd to suppose that man is rational or a knower, and hence a person, only when he is engaged in the act of knowing or so long as his neuro-cortical faculties are developed or unimpaired. Similarly, the prenatal child cannot be said to be less than a person simply because these faculties are in a nascent or inchoate state, for these faculties and their natural potency for development are proper to the nature of the human person.

The developmentalist argument has variations. Consider, for example, biologist Lee M. Silver's approach, which he sets forth in his book, *Remaking Eden*. He draws a distinction between "life" in the *general sense* and in the *special sense*. Although a fertilized human egg is alive and human, it counts as life only in the *general sense* because it lacks the requisite neurological development to count as life in the *special sense*. Only in the sense that donated blood or donated organs are alive and human is the fertilized egg alive and human. Like the single cell fertilized egg, the embryo is clearly alive and clearly human, "but so are the cells that fall off your skin everyday." It, too, falls short of the neurological development that characterizes human life in the *special sense*.

But a massive difference separates individual living things, including human embryos, from their cells and organs. The latter may be alive, but not in the same sense in which an embryo is alive. The embryo is an entity of a specific kind. That specificity demands a particular kind of organization and cells in that they derive their life and meaning from being integral parts of the entity, the proof of which announces itself in this, that when these cells are removed from the entity, they die. The "cells that fall off your skin every day," wither and die.

In its earliest stages, an embryo importantly differs from mere body cells. Even the haploid, single cell though it be, is more than a mere body cell, for it contains the plan that determines its morphological development, that is, the multiplication of cells and their distinctive organization and potentials. That it lacks evidence of neurological activity during the early stages means no more than that the entity's natural potential for neurological activity and later for self-awareness, self-desire, and rationality have yet to be actualized. Nature is economical. Given the embryo's life in the womb, neurological activity, especially in its higher forms of self-awareness and rationality, is not needed. It is logically unwarranted to infer that a human embryo is not a human being or not a person just because those neurological activities are not yet present. There is, after all, no contradiction in the concept of an entity being a human being with the distinctively human powers of reason and self-awareness still to be actualized. Only a functionalist would say that an entity is a human being (or a person) only if it displays, or has displayed in the past, self-awareness and rationality. But that is to offer, what is called in the philosophical trade, a stipulative definition: one stipulates the meaning one is assigning given terms, in this case, that to be a human being, the entity must display certain characteristics.

Approached from another angle, there is a distinction to be observed between the *order of discovery* and the *order of reality*. In the *order of discovery,* we learn what a thing is by observing how it behaves; hence the scholastic formula, *operatio sequitur esse*: operation follows essence. We discover the *order of reality* by following the *order of discovery*: observing that human beings engage in rational activity, we conclude that they are by nature, or essence, rational beings. If we observe no rational activity in an individual born of a human father and a human mother, we would be guilty of an invalid inference were we to conclude that it is, on that count alone, not a human being or a person. To be sure, it might not be a human being but a hydatidiform mole instead. The *Encyclopedia Britannica* tells us that in human pregnancy the hydatidiform mole is an abnormal growth of the chorion that encloses the embryo and is the source of the placenta. The growth of a hydatidiform mole signals either the death or absence of the embryo. The mole is nothing more than an accumulation of cysts, each housing a jellylike substance. Normally, it expels itself from the uterus at about twenty weeks of gestation.

But hydatidiform moles are not the common fruit of pregnancy. What is born to a male and female of the human species is an infant of the human species. And while there can be little doubt that rationality is the most important of human activities, the same observation to which rationality discloses itself also grasps other realities of human nature, such as affectivity, imagination, and emotion. In short, observation reveals that human beings have no rational activities that are not accompanied by feeling and imagining. As asserted above, the observable evidence shows that Aristotle's conception of human nature as rational animal matches human reality far more accurately and completely than does Descartes' conception of man as a thinking being.

Thus, an individual born of a human father and a human mother is, by nature, a human being and a person, even if it is, in the particular case, incapable of rational activity. What has happened, tragically, is that owing to some neurological deficit, caused by genetic anomaly, disease, or externally caused violence, that being has been rendered incapable of the rational activity dictated by his or her essence or nature. What does not follow is Silver's inference that human beings, at their earliest stages of development, exemplify "life in the general sense" rather than "the special sense" just because they do not yet boast a sense of self.

THE WOMAN MUST AFFIRM THE PREGNANCY IN ORDER FOR THE FETUS TO HAVE MORAL SIGNIFICANCE

If this means anything serious at all, it is an appeal to magic. For it implies that by the use of what is in effect an incantation a new entity is created, one that is the subject of primary rights. But affirming that she wants the child to be born means no more than that she wants the child. The motto, "Every child a wanted child," expresses a devoutly desired ideal, but it does not change the reality or the moral status of the unborn. An unwanted child possesses as much dignity and worth as a wanted one. A perusal of the first paragraph of the Declaration of Independence reveals that the natural right tradition upon which our democracy is founded grounds rights proximately in human nature and ultimately in nature's creator, God. Rights, including the right to life, are due human beings because of what they are by nature, not because of what society or the woman sees fit to confer on them.

> We hold these truths to be self-evident, That all men are created equal, that they are endowed by their creator with certain unalienable rights; that among these rights are life, liberty & the pursuit of happiness; that to secure these rights governments are instituted among men, deriving their just powers from the consent of the governed; that whenever any form of government becomes destructive of these ends, it is the right of the people to alter or abolish it, and to institute new government...

MORALLY IRRELEVANT CRITERIA

No less than considerations of skin color, race, religion, intelligence, health or socio-economic circumstances, "stage of development" is a morally irrelevant consideration in relation to primary rights. If it is just as much an unjustifiable homicide to kill an innocent person of color as it is to kill an innocent white person, a poor person as a rich one, a sickly person as a healthy person, it is just as much an unjustifiable homicide deliberately to kill a human fetus as it is to kill deliberately a human infant or adult.

The resort to morally irrelevant criteria to justify the denial of rights to a class of human beings not only constitutes an injustice to the members of that group but to all members of society, including the oppressors. Abraham Lincoln saw that quite clearly in the slavery question, as he asked how a white man could enslave a black man:

> You say A, is white, and B, is black. It is *color*, then; the lighter having the right to enslave the darker? Take care. By this rule, you are to be slave to the first man you meet, with a fairer skin than your own.

> You do not mean *color* exactly?—You mean the whites are *intellectually* the superiors of the blacks, and, therefore have the right to enslave them?

> Take care again. By this rule, you are to be slave to the first man you meet, with an intellect superior to your own.

> But, say you, it is a question of interest; and, if you can make it your *interest*, you have the right to enslave another. Very well. And if he can make it his interest, he has the right to enslave you.

How about a new category of disfavored people: students receiving government loans or philosophy professors with gray hair? My proposals sound ridiculous, but if you think they are too ridiculous, consider the criteria employed by Helga Kuhse and Peter Singer in their book, *Should the Baby Live?*

In the preface, the authors make the bald proposal: "We think that some infants with severe disabilities should be killed." Does this mean that adults with severe disabilities may be killed also? Not exactly. Why not? Because, the authors assure us, different standards of valuation apply.

> For reasons given in later chapters of this book, decisions whether infants should live or die are very different from life and death decisions in the case of people who can understand, or once were capable of understanding, at least some aspects of what a decision to live or die might mean. To put it even more bluntly: it is one thing to say, before a life has properly begun, that such a life should not be lived; it is quite different to say that, once a life is being lived, we need not do our best to improve it. We are sometimes prepared to say the former; we are never prepared to say the latter.

"...[B]efore a life has properly begun," it is permissible to decide "that such a life should not be lived"; whereas one "who can understand, or once ...[was] capable of understanding," owns a life that "has properly begun." This is an exquisite, not to say arbitrary, criterion for deciding matters. Is it to be taken to mean that until the baby can understand, he or she is not a person or a subject of rights in the ontological sense of the Declaration of Independence, to wit, rights are conferred by human nature? Or does it mean that we do not, or should not, assign the same value and importance to babies as subjects of rights and dignity as we do to people who are, or were, capable of understanding? This would be to construe rights in the social rather than natural sense.

If the authors mean "properly" to be taken in the ontological sense, their position is quite weak, for they haven't shown, or even tried to show, that the difference between one who has yet to reach the stage of understanding and one who has reached it is substantial enough to warrant establishing a difference of kind rather than a mere difference of degree. Only if babies differ *in kind* from people who can understand and think can you, on the one hand, justify killing them while, on the other, condemn killing other humans. As pointed out above, this is the kind of distinction that we make when we wish morally or legally to disenfranchise a disfavored group of people, as, for example, in the *Dred Scott* decision and Hitler's Nuremberg Declaration on the Jews. But this requires showing that you can have human beings who are not persons, and that, as I've argued already, is not an easy thing to do. The authors do seem to imply such a view in their distinction between humans who cannot yet understand and humans who do understand or have understood. For this bespeaks the functionalist conception of personhood as opposed to the substantialist or essentialist conception.

But the fact that they have seen fit to include in the group who have attained a life "properly lived" those who are no longer capable of understanding along with the fact that they have not seen fit to pursue the functionalist/substantialist distinction lead me to suspect that they have in mind some social sense of "properly." I say "some" social sense because it is far from clear that society values people who can no longer understand better than severely afflicted newborns. The current debate over physician-assisted suicide and even over the involuntary euthanasia of certain classes of the elderly suggests to me that society finds the incompetent elderly at least as burdensome as severely afflicted newborns.

This is but one more example of the mercurial nature of any social sense of what is proper. I understand that the most serious obstacle in the way of legalizing euthanasia in Japan is that culture's traditional reverence for the elderly. In contrast, the United States idolizes the young while harboring ambiguous sentiments towards the elderly, as evidenced by the patronizing term, "senior citizen." What's wrong with being just elderly or old or aged? Such variation verifies Lincoln's warning about using morally irrelevant criteria. It is just as much an act of murder to kill deliberately an innocent baby, albeit a severely afflicted one, as it is to kill deliberately an innocent, normal, healthy, adult. Once resort to criteria like "a life properly lived," then Pandora's Box is opened. Who is to decide what a "life properly lived" is? Pol Pot of Cambodia gave the order to kill men wearing eyeglasses for fear that they were intellectuals.

THE DIFFERENCE BETWEEN THE HUMAN UNBORN AND CHIMPANZEES

It's pretty common for pro-lifers to defend the unborn's right to life by calling attention to its forty-six chromosomes and the morphological process directed by the DNA code. This has been greeted in some quarters with the question, "So what? There is about 3 percent difference between the DNA of a human being and that of a chimpanzee; almost 97 per cent of the DNA is the same. With such a small margin of difference, what makes you think that the appeal to the fetus's chromosomal structure confers a right to life on it and not on chimpanzees?"

I'd like to respond to this objection by proposing two versions of the paragraph from the *Declaration of Independence* that I've already favored with two citations in this chapter.

> We hold these truths to be self-evident, That all men are
> created equal, that they are endowed by their creator
> with certain unalienable rights; that among these are life,

liberty & the pursuit of happiness; that to secure these rights governments are instituted among men, deriving their just powers from the consent of the governed; that whenever any form of government becomes destructive of these ends, it is the right of people to alter or abolish it, and to institute new government, laying its foundation on such principles and organizing its powers in such form, as to them shall seem most likely to reflect their safety and happiness.

There are 110 words in this paragraph. Suppose we add one word, "not," so that the opening line now reads, "We hold these truths *not* to be self-evident..." There is less than one percent difference between the two paragraphs and yet the difference in meaning between them is infinite. They are, in fact, contrary positions. Because the whole of the Declaration of Independence depends on the validity of the claim that it is self-evidently true that human beings possesses the inalienable rights it lists therein, the addition of the word "not" constitutes a much smaller difference between the altered version of the document and its original, making that difference the merest fraction of one percent. Yet, as this difference becomes smaller and smaller the actual difference in the meaning of the two documents becomes ever larger.

How can the difference in percentage be so small and the difference in meaning be so huge? The answer is that the percentage of difference represents the document reduced to its quantitative units; it is an abstraction. But it is far more than an aggregation of units. The whole of the *Declaration of Independence* is one complex idea, an integrated totality formed by the organization of its parts, to wit, its arguments, theories, concepts, assertions, all of which are directed to a single end, the creation of that single, complex but unified idea – a compelling justification for a people's right to revolt against an unauthorized and oppressive ruler.

Admittedly, the quantification of things produces valuable results, as in statistical analysis, physics and, preeminently, pure mathematics. But this should not allow us to lose sight of the fact that the picture of reality created by quantification is an abstraction whose only direct counterpart in the real world is the quantity in bodies. Consider, for example, how mathematics defines a "line": "that which has length but neither width nor depth"; or a "point": that which has neither length, nor width, nor depth, but is the intersection of two lines." Find something, anything, in the world that doesn't have all three – length, width, and depth. For all its importance, the fact remains that quantification offers us only a partial view of reality and if taken as the standard of our knowledge of it, becomes an outright distortion of it.

There is no problem in talking about the difference between human beings and chimpanzees in terms of their DNA, but that is quite different from saying that the difference between the two species is reducible to their respective kinds and percentages of DNA. Again, that is an abstraction, which, although valuable in its own domain, distorts, if pressed, the reality of both human beings and chimpanzees.

CHAPTER SEVEN

"HE'S NOT A PHYSICIAN!"

...'"post tenebras spero lucem' – After darkness I await the light."
The Adventures of Don Quixote, Pt.II, Ch.LXVIII

I confess to having had hardly any debates in which the subject of partial-birth abortion came up. No matter. The memoirs of an abortion-debater would be glaringly incomplete without some mention of it. Until my last couple of debates over at the University of California, I avoided mentioning partial-birth abortion because I feared that the Berkeley audience would interpret a description of the procedure, given its grisly nature, as a transparent resort to emotionalism. But a couple of years ago, someone in the audience asked me to address the topic. Before I could start my presentation, my opponent jumped in, with the warning, "He's not a physician!" Up until then, this representative of a local Planned Parenthood clinic, was mild mannered and anything but aggressive. In fact, before the class began, she said that, rather than have a debate, she would prefer that each of us simply present our respective positions. So why the abrupt, bordering on the strident, "He's not a physician"? Clearly, she knew that any accurate description of the procedure would inevitably focus attention on the murderous nature of abortion. From then on, I resolved always to include partial-birth abortion among the topics of my anti-abortion presentation.

So grisly a procedure deserves an explanation. But I'd like to lead into my attempt to explain it by sharing with the reader an interpretation of the wholesale abortions going on in the United States, not to mention in the rest of the Western world. I use the exclusionary term, "Western world," because the Judeo-Christian tradition of the West acknowledges incalculable intrinsic worth in every human being and, accordingly, unreservedly condemns the deliberate killing of the innocent.

While I'm at it, I should also clarify the clause, "...unreservedly condemns the deliberate killing of the innocent." We in the Western world have a spotty record when it comes to respecting the dignity and rights of our fellow human beings. Having made a great to-do about the Declaration of Independence in the previous chapter, what am I to say about the United States' justification of slavery, treatment of Native Americans, and in World War II firebombing Dresden and Tokyo, dropping atomic bombs on Hiroshima and Nagasaki, all of which bombings were deliberate killings of thousands of defenseless civilians? You don't have to look any further for examples of how spectacularly short we fell from our professed principles. My answer is that these examples bespeak a combination of fallibility and moral weakness. Books like Carl Becker's *The Declaration of Independence*, and Joseph J. Ellis' *The Founding Brothers* reveal the contradiction the founders of our nation recognized between "life, liberty, and the pursuit of happiness," and the ownership of slaves, but, for various reasons, couldn't bring themselves to condemn slavery: they and their colleagues were, after all, slave owners; and some, like Jefferson, were convinced that a condemnation of slavery in the *Declaration* would destroy its chances of passage in the assembly, while others, like Washington, believed the institution of slavery to be immoral but also believed that it was so intimately tied to the economy that banning it would cause economic disaster.

But unless one is a psychopath, it's very hard to admit to yourself that the beings you're oppressing and exploiting are your ontological and thus moral equals. So to be able to look at yourself squarely each morning as you gaze at the mirror, you must create the mythology that the beings you enslave are somehow not really moral entities, not persons. Human beings they may be, but occupying a lower rung on the human ladder. Hardly surprising, then, that the United States Supreme Court, in its infamous Dred Scot decision, claimed that Blacks were only 3/5 persons according to the *Constitution*. And our assessment of Native Americans was similar. In his essay, "When Do People Begin?," Germain Grisez captures our mercurial use of the word "person" by recounting an historical event: "Chief

Standing Bear of the Poncas became a person in April 1879 by a court decision rejecting the U.S. district attorney's contention that the Chief was not a person 'within the meaning of the law.' The following month, when Standing Bear's brother, Big Snake, tried to leave the reservation, General Sherman pointed out that the decision about Standing Bear applied only to him, and Big Snake was shot to death while resisting arrest."

The above examples show how inclined we are to cheat at solitaire. We try to deceive ourselves into thinking that the groups of humans we disfavor deserve nothing better than we allow them. We have defined them out of the community of persons, thereby creating a category of disposable human beings. That's exactly what we've done to unborn human beings and what we are currently trying to do with the elderly and infirm. Since I've already emphasized my reluctance to take seriously the arguments advanced by the pro-abortionists' attempts to show that the fetus is not a human being, a person, a subject of rights, or possessed of moral significance greater than that of the members of other mammalian species, I herein speculate on the underlying motive for abortion and especially for elective abortions.

PARTIAL-BIRTH ABORTION IN TEN BLOODY STEPS

That speculation draws increased plausibility from the current debate over "partial-birth abortion." "Dilatation and Extraction (D & X) is the medical term for the procedure, but a description of it shows that "partial-birth abortion" accurately describes what it does. In the Fall, 1993 edition of *Cincinnati Medicine*, W. Martin Haskell, M.D., the practitioner who introduced the D & X procedure, was interviewed in response to readers' inquiries regarding the controversial method for second trimester abortion. The doctor's step-by-step description appeared on page 19 as part of that interview:

The D & X Procedure – Dilation and Extraction, (D & X), a method for second trimester abortion up to 26 weeks, was developed in 1992 by Cincinnati physician W. Martin Haskell, M.D. It is a modification of Dismemberment and Extraction (D & E), which has been used in the U.S. since the 1970s. Haskell has performed more than 700 D & X procedures in his office.

Step One—The patient's cervix is dilated to 9-11 mm over a period of two days using Dilapan hydroscopic dilators. The patient remains at home during the dilation period.

Step Two—In the operating room, patients are given Valium, the Dilapan are removed and the cervix is scrubbed, anesthetized and grasped with a tenaculum. Membranes are ruptured.

Step Three—The surgical assistant scans the fetus with ultrasound, locating the lower extremities.

Step Four—Using a large forcep, the surgeon opens and closes its jaws to firmly grasp a lower extremity. The surgeon turns the fetus if necessary and pulls the extremity into the vagina.

Step Five—The surgeon uses his fingers to deliver the opposite lower extremity, then the torso, shoulders, and upper extremities.

Step Six—The skull lodges at the internal cervical os. Usually there is not enough dilation for it to pass through. The fetus is spine up.

Step Seven—A right-handed surgeon slides the fingers of his left hand along the back of the fetus and hooks the shoulders of the fetus with the index and ring fingers (palm down). He slides the tip of his middle finger along the spine towards the skull while applying traction to the shoulder and lower extremities. The middle finger lifts and pushes the anterior cervical lip out of the way.

Step Eight—While maintaining this tension, the surgeon takes a pair of blunt curved scissors in the right hand. He advances the tip, curved down, along the spine and under his middle finger until he feels it contact the base of the skull under the tip of his middle finger. The surgeon forces the scissors into the base of the skull and spreads the scissors to enlarge the opening.

Step Nine—The surgeon removes the scissors and introduces a suction catheter into this hole and evacuates the skull contents.

Step Ten— With the catheter still in place, he applies traction to the fetus, removing it completely from the patient, then removes the placenta.

Why leave the baby's head in the cervix? Whatever may be the medical reasons, there is a non-medical, very practical reason for doing so. According to Federal law and the laws of all fifty states, a baby delivered completely from the vagina is considered a live birth; so killing it would be homicide. But, if the baby's head is left in the cervix, then it's just another kind of abortion. If this is not infanticide, then there is no such thing.

A common interpretation of the pro-abortionists' reluctance to condemn this grisly procedure is that they know, despite their pronouncements to the contrary, that human life is a continuum from conception until death. They accordingly understand the logic of this continuum: if you can make abortion illegal at the later stages (18 to 26 weeks is when partial-birth abortions are performed), then there is no inconsistency in making abortion illegal during the earlier stages. Given the particularly horrible nature of partial-birth abortion, the intransigence of the pro-abortionists regarding it, suggests a motive much darker than the announced one of protecting women's reproductive rights. In 1997 and '98, Congress passed, by an overwhelming margin in both the House and Senate, the "Partial-Birth Abortion Ban Act." If passed into law, the bill would punish physicians performing the procedure by fine or imprisonment. The bill made an exception for partial-birth abortions "necessary to save the life of a mother whose life is endangered by a physical disorder, illness, or injury." Both times, President Clinton vetoed the bill, claiming that it contained no allowance for doing partial-birth abortions to preserve the mother's health.

There are at least three important things wrong with the mother's health provision. The first goes back to the U.S. Supreme Court's *Doe v. Bolton* decision of 1973, which defines "health" to mean "all factors – physical, emotional, psychological, familial, and the woman's age – relevant to the well-being of the patient." If President Clinton's health provision were added to the bill, it would justify, under this definition of "health," any and all partial-birth abortions. It would, in short, practically nullify the bill.

Second, the vast majority of partial-birth abortions are blatantly elective, having nothing to do with any clinical understanding of "health." According to the November 20th, 1995 edition of *American Medical News*, "Dr. Haskell conceded that 80% of his late-term abortions were elective." In a transcript of an *American Medical News* interview, he said that the remaining 20% were performed "probably" "for genetic reasons." So the only way the health of the mother figures in 100% of the late-term abortions he performs is the absurd sense of "health" handed down in *Doe v. Bolton*. And Dr. McMahon, the nation's leading provider of late-term abortions until his death, "…said he would not do an elective abortion after 26 weeks. In a chart he released to the House Judiciary Committee, 'depression' was listed most often as the reason for late-term abortions with maternal indications. 'Clef lip' was listed nine times under fetal indications."

It's usually during the fifth and sixth months that the method of partial-birth abortion is used, but Dr. James McMahon admitted using it for abortions in the third trimester, that is, the seventh and eighth months. The July 5, 1993 edition of the *American Medical News* writes that he does abortions "through all 40 weeks of pregnancy." In 1995, he informed the House Judiciary Committee in writing that he performed such abortions during the third trimester on babies that had no "flaw" at all for reasons such as the mother's youth or for "psychiatric" problems. McMahon further admitted that one-fourth of the babies he aborted well into the seventh month had no flaws whatsoever. McMahon said that of the approximately 2000 partial-birth abortions he performed, only 9% were performed for "maternal [health] indications," and then the most common reason was "depression."

Third, the claim that the procedure is sometimes necessary to protect the mother from serious physical injury is massively suspect. In a letter sent to Senator Rick Santorum (R-Pa.) dated May 19, 1997, P. John Seward, M.D., the Executive Vice-President of the American Medical Association wrote, "Thank you for the opportunity to work with you towards restricting *a procedure we all agree is not good medicine*." (Italics added). "Physicians Ad Hoc Coalition for Truth" ("PHACT"), an organization numbering more than 500 physicians (predominantly specializing in obstetrics, perinatology, and allied disciplines) released a fact statement challenging the claim that some women require partial-birth abortions to avoid grave physical harm: "*We, and many other doctors across the United States, regularly treat women whose unborn children suffer these and other serious conditions. Never is the partial-birth procedure medically indicated. Rather, such infants are regularly and safely delivered live, vaginally, with no threat to the mother's health or fertility.*" In concert with other PHACT members, former Surgeon General, C. Everett Koop, stated, in writing, that "partial-birth abortion is never medically necessary to protect the mother's medical health or her future fertility. On the contrary, this procedure can pose a significant threat to both."

If the vast majority of partial-birth abortions are elective, the question arises, "Why do women wait so long to have an abortion? " Sometimes the woman and the man separate and the woman decides she doesn't wish to bear the child or a teenage girl hides her pregnancy from her parents until she starts "showing."

FETAL PAIN

I said above that partial-birth abortion is a grisly procedure. All abortions are, but this procedure is especially grisly, a fact that its defenders would prefer remained secret. The July 5, 1993 edition of the *American Medical News* quotes an abortion federation statement that appeared in the Morrisville, Vt. *Transcript:* "The fetus is dead 24 hours before the pictured procedure is undertaken." "The pictured procedure" refers to the moment, focused on by opponents of the procedure, when the surgeon plunges a pair of surgical scissors into the base of the baby's skill and then inserts an aspirator to suck out its brains, thus collapsing its skull. Kate Michelman, president of the National Abortion and Reproductive Rights Action League, along with columnist Ellen Goodman, professed the view that the anesthesia given the mother kills the child so that it suffers no pain from partial-birth abortion. But Dr. Haskell told the *American Medical News* that "the majority of the fetuses aborted this way are alive until the end of the procedure. On March 26th, in a statement given before the Congressional Subcommittee on the Constitution, Dr. Norig Ellison, then President of the American Society of Anesthesiologists, contradicted the claim, which he attributes to Dr. McMahon, "that anesthesia given to the mother as part of dilatation and extraction abortion procedure eliminates any pain to the fetus and that a medical coma is induced in the fetus, causing a 'neurological fetal demise,' or – in lay terms – 'brain death'." On the contrary, Dr. Ellison continued:

> Although it is certainly true that some general analgesic medications given to the mother will reach the fetus and perhaps provide some pain relief, it is equally true that pregnant women are routinely heavily sedated during the second or third trimester for the performance of a variety of necessary surgical procedures with absolutely no adverse effect on the fetus, let alone death or 'brain death.' In my medical judgment, it would be necessary – in order to achieve 'neurological demise' of the fetus in a 'partial-birth' abortion – to anesthetize the mother to such a degree as to place her own health in serious jeopardy.

If the unborn baby is not killed, rendered insensate or brain dead by the anesthetic administered to the mother, then we have to address the issue of fetal pain. In her testimony before the same Congressional subcommittee, Dr. Jean A Wright, Division Director of Pediatric Critical Care & Emergency Medicine at Emory University School of Medicine, called attention to the current scientific data on the perception of pain in the human fetus and neonate, from which she drew the following conclusions:

> The scientific literature reviewed above and my clinical experience in the delivery of general anesthesia, systematic analgesia, conscious sedation, local and regional anesthesia to a wide variety of patients lead me to believe that:
>
> 1. The anatomical and functional processes responsible for the perception of pain have developed in human fetuses that may be considered for 'partial-birth abortions.' (At this stage of neurologic development, human fetuses respond to the pain caused by needle puncture *in utero* in a similar manner as older children or adults, within the limits of their behavioral repertoire.)

It is likely that the threshold for such pain perception is lower than that of older preterm newborns, full-term newborns, and older age groups. Thus, the pain experienced during 'partial-birth abortions' by the human fetus would have a much greater intensity than any similar procedures performed in older age groups.

[Dr. Wright bases this conclusion on the following points established in the scientific literature: (1) Contrary to the traditional understanding, the lack of myelination (i.e., the layer around the nerve fibers) does not prevent neonates and infants from perceiving pain; 2) the Cutaneous Flexor Reflex shows a lower threshold to pain stimulation in preterm neonates than in term neonates and adults; 3) studies of neurotransmitting substances in the spinal cord; 4) receptors for pain in the fetal brain; 5) pain and stress reflected in the hormones produced by the fetus; 6) pharmacokinetic studies of anesthetic drugs show that higher plasma concentrations are required to maintain effective surgical anesthesia in preterm neonates as compared to old age groups.]

2. Current methods for providing maternal anesthesia during 'partial-birth abortions' are unlikely to prevent the experience of pain and stress in the human fetuses before their death occurs after partial delivery.

Given the scientific literature on human fetal and neonatal perception of pain, I have to observe that partial-birth abortionists, like Dr. Haskell, either know about this literature or they do not. If they know about it, they willingly engage in an elective procedure that not only kills an innocent human being but causes it considerable pain as well. If they don't know about it, shame on them still, for they have a professional responsibility to remain current on the scientific literature that directly pertains to the surgical procedures they perform.

And, given their pro-abortion predilections, the media have remained predictably silent on this issue. But imagine the fuss they would make if they found out that Dr. Haskell and the other "partial-birth" abortionists were causing similar pain to cats and dogs. Of course, "liberals" tread cautiously around their own sacred cows, especially when it comes to "women's reproductive rights" or "abortion rights." Never mind that the exercise of such putative rights requires the deliberate killing of unborn babies as well as the infliction of pain.

WHO ARE THE VIOLENT PEOPLE?

The appeals to "reproductive rights" are nothing more than attempts to breathe a halo around what is, to borrow the words of the Catholic Church's Second Vatican Council, "an unspeakable crime." Induced abortion offers itself as an efficient way to end unwanted pregnancies, even though it involves a procedure as grisly as partial-birth abortion. How did we get to this point? Maybe we were never far from it; after all, we had to fight a civil war in the 19th century to get rid of legalized slavery. But I'm partial to the explanation of gratuitous violence offered by the late forensic psychiatrist, Fredric Wertham. In his book, *A Sign for Cain*, he challenged the view that only the demented, the dregs, and the gangsters perpetrate violence, especially in its more horrendous forms. An example of what he means by "gratuitous violence" would be teenagers dropping boulders off of freeway overpasses onto the automobiles below, killing their drivers. He goes so far as to challenge the widely accepted view that women who batter their babies are emotionally disturbed. To be sure, some of them are disturbed, he agrees, but not the majority. The correct explanation is that most women batter their babies because violence is an increasingly acceptable way to handle frustration.

To support his claim that violence is not the preserve of the demented or gangster class, Wertham devotes two chapters to the euthanasia murders in Germany. It turns out that the majority of the physicians and psychiatrists who managed the extermination of prisoners and children were renowned members of the medical community. Wertham's book can thus be seen as an evocation of the principle, "Handsome is as handsome does" rather than "Handsome does as handsome is." Their otherwise respectable lives, high social station, and medical achievements in no way mitigated the morally outrageous behavior of these physicians.

Equally, the act of plunging surgical scissors into an unborn baby's skull to make an opening to insert an aspiration tube to suck out its brains and collapse its skull is not the less grisly because performed by licensed physicians in good standing with the medical profession. True, the vast majority of the Unites States Congress voted to outlaw this procedure, but President Clinton's veto produced no public outrage, largely, no doubt, because the media chose not to show the American people just what partial-birth abortion involves. But if a Dr. Kevorkian or a teenager, especially one from the inner city, had collapsed the skull of a human fetus and sucked out its brains, the media would have made publicizing the procedure a priority.

What it comes down to is that killing unborn babies has become a socially acceptable way to end an inconvenient pregnancy and killing them by partial-birth abortion has become a socially acceptable way to end an inconvenient late-stage pregnancy, despite its monstrous nature.

A CLASS OF DISPOSABLE PEOPLE

Time after time, this attitude confronts me in my abortion debates at the University of California. Consider the following two recent examples, both from the same session. A woman, in her late thirties, sitting in the first row of the large Berkeley auditorium said: "Anyone who has studied embryology knows that you're right when you say the fetus is a human being from the moment of conception. I have two children and I've had two abortions. Abortion is necessary to protect women from male hegemony." Given her affirmation that the fetus is a human being, her subsequent claim that "abortion is necessary to protect women from male hegemony" translates into an admission that it is necessary to kill unborn human beings. Later in the session, a college-age female commented: "Your science and logic are correct, but you ignore the sociology of the sixteen year old girl whose life will be ruined if she has the baby." The implication of this statement is that the fetus is a human being (my "science and logic are correct"), but it's all right to kill that innocent human being to prevent the pregnant sixteen year old's life from being "ruined."

I find it remarkable that people can, on the one hand, affirm that the fetus is a human being and, on the other, justify killing it, especially for rhetorical reasons, such as "male hegemony" and the "sociology" of the pregnant teenager. The majority of abortions are not performed as a defense against male hegemony or as protection from the "sociology" of teenage pregnancy. They are performed as a means of birth control, though it is birth control *after the fact*, to be sure. No matter. If it is acceptable to kill a human being in the womb for these reasons, surely it cannot be unacceptable to kill a human being in the womb by partial-birth abortion. The point being that, if the timing of the pregnancy is intolerable, then any legal means of ending it must be all right.

Given this attitude toward induced abortion, the spectacularly grisly nature of partial-birth abortion apparently shouldn't allow one to get too squeamish. Although confessing to mixed feelings about the procedure, Dr. McMahon, according to the November 20, 1995 edition of *Medical News*, seemed to have little trouble resolving those feelings.

'I have two positions that may be internally inconsistent, and that's probably why I fight with this all the time,' he said.

> 'I do have moral compunctions. And if I see a case that's later, like after 20 weeks where it frankly is a child to me, I really agonize over it because the potential is so eminently there. I think, "Gee, it's too bad that this child couldn't be adopted."'
>
> 'On the other hand, I have another position, which I think is superior in the hierarchy of questions, and that is: "Who owns the child?" It's got to be the mother.'

This clear admission that the mother possesses the moral credentials to kill her child is couched under the legal rubric, "the right to privacy," under the social rubric, "choice," and "protection against male hegemony" under the feminist rubric, and "otherwise the girl's life will be ruined" under the hard case rubric. They can all be boiled down to a single rubric: "Do unto others and then clear out." When it comes to abortion, "Do unto others" means "I have the right to kill unborn children when they stand in my way"; and "then clear out" means create rhetoric to hide the fact that you've deliberately killed an innocent human being.

The hubris in this outlook is undeniable. Permit me to illustrate this with the following imaginary dialogue. I say "imaginary" because you simply don't get the opportunity to engage a member of your audience in dialogue.

Pro–abortionist: A sixteen year-old girl who can't get an abortion would have to drop out of high school, never get to college, and might end up on welfare. Her whole life would be ruined.

Anti–abortionist: Since her "whole life would be ruined," would you recommend, then, that she kill herself?

Pro–abortionist: No, of course, not.

Anti–abortionist: Why not? With a "ruined" life in prospect, what's left if she goes on living?

Pro–abortionist: The girl would have some hope of getting back on track.

Anti–abortionist: But suppose her odds of getting back on track are zero or close to it. Would you say then that she'd be better off dead? That she should kill herself?

Pro–abortionist: You can never be sure that a person's life won't improve, especially when it's a youngster with all those years still ahead.

Anti–abortionist: Well, just for the sake of argument, let's look at it in a purely theoretical way and say that we know for sure that if that sixteen year old girl had the baby, she'd never graduate from high school and would be a welfare mom for the rest of her life. Then would you say that she'd be better off dead; that she should kill herself?

Pro–abortionist: In the first place, a purely theoretical case has no bearing on real life and real people. In the real world, there's no way you can be sure that a person's life won't improve. And in the second place, even if we could predict that she'd be a welfare mom for the rest of her life, she'd still be better off alive than dead.

Anti–abortionist: Are you saying that even a "ruined" life is better than being dead?

Pro–abortionist: Yes.

Anti–abortionist: You're saying, then, that life is more valuable than graduating from high school, going to college, having a career, etc.?

Pro–abortionist: Obviously it is.

Anti–abortionist: One thing perplexes me. You say that the sixteen year old single mother, no matter how dim her prospects, would not be better off dead because nobody can be sure that her life won't improve and that even if we could be sure, her life would still be worth living because life is more valuable than education, success, etc.

Pro–abortionist: Yes, but what's perplexing about that?

Anti–abortionist: Just this. If life is so valuable, then why do you say that a pregnant sixteen-year-old girl should have an abortion to keep from ruining her life? Earlier you agreed that, from the moment of conception, the fetus is a human being. And since, therefore, induced abortion is the deliberate killing of an innocent human being, do you believe that the sixteen year old girl's life is worth keeping because her life is more precious than things like economic self-sufficiency, education, and professional success, but the unborn child's life is not more precious than her economic self-sufficiency, education, and professional success?

Pro–abortionist: Yes, but you can't compare the life of a sixteen year old with that of a fetus. The girl's already got a life: a self-identity, family, friends, and goals. The fetus has none of these things.

Anti–abortionist: So you're saying that all human lives are not equally valuable.

Pro–abortionist: That's right. There's something absurd about equating a fetus with a human being who's already had a life outside the womb.

Anti–abortionist: Then, when you say that life is more precious than economic self-sufficiency, education, professional success, etc., you don't really mean, by "life," "life itself" but "life at a certain stage of development" or "life in certain situations."

Pro–abortionist: I think that's pretty obvious.

Anti–abortionist: Am I safe in saying, then, that you agree with Singer's justification for killing a newborn based on the distinction between "before a life has properly begun" and "once a life is being lived"?

Pro–abortionist: I think it's a valid distinction. You can't equate a fetus' life with that of a sixteen-year-old girl.

Anti–abortionist: So, in order to prevent her life from being derailed by the birth of a baby out of wedlock, it would be morally permissible for the girl to kill her unborn child. From all you've said, your position on the primacy of life over other things is this: It's *my* life that has primacy over education, economic self-sufficiency, professional status, etc, and not necessarily anyone else's life. If human life itself enjoyed primacy over these other things, then it would be immoral deliberately to kill an unborn child to keep one's own life on track. But if, at the end of the day, it's just *my* life that counts — and that's what seems to be your underlying premise — then that would explain how you can, on the one hand, uphold the primacy of life and justify induced abortion, on the other.

Pro–abortionist: You've left out an important ingredient. I said several times that there's no comparison between a fetus and someone who's living outside the womb. The sixteen-year-old girl has self-identify, personal plans and goals, family and friends. The fetus has none of these. So my claim that she has the moral right to abort her fetus in order to remain in high school doesn't lead —as you say it does — to the conclusion that *her life alone* enjoys primacy but that her life enjoys primacy over fetal life.

Anti–abortionist: I could understand that position if you held that the fetus was not a human being. But since you agree that, from the moment of conception, it is a human being, how can you maintain that the moral right to kill an unborn human being is not also the right to kill already born human beings? After all, we're not talking about a difference of kind but of degree. As the late philosopher, Yves R. Simon, observed, it's just as much an act of murder to kill a sickly man as it is to kill a healthy one; a poor man as a rich man; a black man as a white man; and just as much an act of murder to kill a human fetus as it is to kill a child or an adult. Simon's point is that the circumstances of human life — economic, physical, social, developmental — have no bearing on whether a particular act of killing is murder for the simple reason that they do not determine whether the life they surround is a human life. And it is the deliberate killing of an innocent human being that determines whether a particular act of killing counts as murder.

The dialogue between the pro-abortionist and the anti-abortionist is over. As the creator of the dialogue, I claim the prerogative to end it as suddenly as I started it. My point in engaging the pro-abortionist who placed so much stock in the "sociology" of the pregnant sixteen year old girl was to use some drama to get across the truth that the legalization of induced abortion signaled the creation of a new class of human beings, "disposable humans." We can hardly deny that the fetus is a human being, but we claim the right to dispose of that human being (oops! I meant "fetus") when we deem its conception inconvenient.

The horrendous fact is that abortion is regarded by so many today as legitimate because it's a relatively easy way to rid oneself, under social and medical auspices, of an inconvenient pregnancy, especially so since the woman doesn't see her victim. It's thus easy to conceal the truth that induced abortion is the direct killing of an innocent human being. But, as shown above, the procedure known as "partial-birth abortion" dramatically calls attention to the savagery of induced abortion. Thanks to bioethicists like Peter Singer and Michael Tooley, infanticide is also justifiable. This makes sense when you bear in mind that mammalian reproduction is characterized by continuity of development. If it's permissible to kill before birth, it's permissible to kill after birth.

Notice that we've not stopped with infanticide but have moved to killing adults, under such rubrics as "death with dignity" and "the right to die." What abortion, infanticide, and physician-assisted suicide have in common is that they are all ways of killing people who, we have decided, are better off dead. As I emphasized in the previous chapter, reasons like "stage of human development" and "a life not yet properly lived" are morally irrelevant criteria for distinguishing between justifiable and unjustifiable homicide. Anyone who thinks they morally justify the deliberate killing of unborn babies, infants, or elderly and infirmed people, will be hard-pressed to point to a line of demarcation between killing the unborn or deformed and the chronically unemployed.

CHAPTER EIGHT

THE VAMPIRE'S KISS

"Out with you, malignant enchanters! Out with you, sorcerers' rabble! For I am Don Quixote de la Mancha, against whom your evil intentions are futile and devoid of any power."

The Adventures of Don Quixote, Pt. II, Ch. XLVI

Catchy title, no? My long career of debating and thinking about abortion has shaped the thoughts set forth below. They offer a mythic interpretation of the cultural apology for killing the unborn. The event that finalized in my mind the connection between induced abortion and vampirism occurred about ten years ago with the media reports of fetal tissue transplants.

So far as I know, the only vampires whose existence has been verified are the small winged mammals, indigenous to South America, that feed off the blood of cattle and horses. Despite the vampiric behavior of Countess Elizabeth Bathory in the 16th century and Ann Rice's talents for portraying human vampires so vividly and congenially that they might be the folks down the street, claims about real human vampires have not managed to withstand scrutiny. But when former President Clinton's Bioethics Advisory Committee recommended Federal funding for embryo stem cell transfer, I got to wondering if the vampire doesn't enjoy a mythic presence in our culture, a presence that is exerting an ever-increasing influence on our thinking about life and death and the meaning of human existence.

BLOOD TIES

How does the myth connect with the real world? I discern a clue to the connection in an observation offered by McNally and Florescu in their book, *In Search of Dracula*. The authors write that although it is not the historical Dracula but the mythical Dracula that exerts such compelling force on our imaginations, the reality and the fantasy are tied together by blood – the bloodthirsty actions of the historical Dracula and the insatiable hunger for blood of the mythical Dracula. Thus the connection I see between the vampire myth and contemporary society is blood, the blood of the innocent spilled by our abortion culture and our reasons for spilling it. Despite the humanitarian facade presented by apostles of embryo stem cell transfer (now referred to as the morally neutral "esc") as they tell about its promise of curing the ailments of mankind and retrieving lost youth, it remains a grisly, dehumanizing procedure: it requires the destruction of the unborn since the stem cells must be harvested from aborted fetuses or embryos discarded in the process of *in vitro* fertilization.

Although our rapidly increasing success with adult stem cells promises to eliminate the attractiveness of embryo stem cells, the use of the latter continues, along with the demand for increased government funding. Besides, the current movement to clone human beings warns us, if the attempts succeed, that many cloned human beings will be subjects of human experimentation, the aim of which will be to improve our human existence – another example of employing life-draining techniques on some humans to perpetuate the lives of other humans.

So we're being invited to accept the killing of unborn, newborn, and cloned human beings to make ourselves healthier, younger, and more vital. If this isn't vampirism, nothing is; for the essential characteristic of the vampire, in the cultures of east and west, is draining life from another for one's own benefit.

BOURGEOIS VAMPIRES

How does Dracula gain respectability? It's not as hard as you may think. First of all, he doesn't have to look monstrous and terrifying, at least not all the time. Not only, according to vampiric lore, does the vampire possess powers to change himself into other forms – dogs, cats, bats, wolves, and even smoke, but in Bram Stoker's novel, *Dracula,* Count Dracula walks the streets of London in broad daylight, wearing his straw hat and looking like any other man. So he can look normal and perhaps even congenial. But attaining social respectability by sheer force of will is beyond his powers. The folklore and literary traditions tell us that the vampire cannot get to his victims all on his own; he needs their cooperation, for he cannot cross the threshold of their lives unless they invite him to cross. Consider the words of Twitchell:

> The vampire never wantonly destroys – in fact, his initial victims are preordained; they are those whom he loved most when alive. The initial victims are friends and family who, of course, recognize the vampire as one who was loved and trusted. This recognition is important, for the vampire cannot pick and choose on his own; rather he must be picked, "invited" into the relationship. The victim, not consciously realizing that the friend or relative is the devil in disguise, understandably and ironically obliges.

> ...the victim must make some inviting move; she must unclasp the window, open the door, do anything that shows she is acceding, even slightly. This crucial point is repeated in almost all the literary adaptations, for the vampire cannot cross a threshold without this invitation; he is bound to wait pathetically like a schoolboy until invited in. Once inside, however, his powers gradually increase. He is still not in control and so must attempt to entrance her with his hypnotic stare, for his powers are initially ocular, like those of many monsters...This trance, if successful, will put the victim under his power...

Who grants the vampire admission into society? I suggest that the leader class does. By the "leader class" I mean intellectuals, academics, journalists, judges, attorneys, legislators, clergy, and physicians. The leader class welcomes the vampire by its falsehoods and obfuscations.

ABORTION DECEITS

For example, feminists – clearly members of the leader class insofar as they represent the white intelligentsia – are always telling us anti-abortionists to keep our hands off their bodies. Laws forbidding elective abortions are, they insist, nothing less than government interference in that most sacred of possessions, one's body. But they don't seem to see any contradiction in their admonitions about bodily integrity when they elect, using a hit man dressed in white robes, to encroach on the bodily integrity of another, to dismember their unborn.

You might suppose that they don't see any contradiction because they think the fetus is part of their body or some kind of subhuman parasite rather than a separate human life. But I've never been able to bring myself to believe that the apologists for abortion think that the unborn is anything less than a human being and a *bona fide* subject of rights. This is not just a hunch or persistent intuition. It's all the things that I've brought forward in the previous chapters that leave me otherwise unable to explain why my debate opponents have assiduously ducked discussions about the humanity of the fetus, why the media so carefully refer to the unborn as a "fetus" when the context is what it presumptuously calls "abortion rights," but yet unabashedly says "unborn child" when the context is an intrauterine surgical intervention that saves the unborn. It's not as if asking whether the unborn is a human being and, therefore, if induced abortion is the deliberate killing of a human being were "off the wall" questions or improbable speculations. After all, we are talking about a being that is the product of a human father and a human mother. It seems to me eminently reasonable to ask, "If the fetus is not a human being, then what is it?"

Academic apologists for abortion do, to be sure, address the humanity and personhood of the fetus, but I confess to finding their arguments contrived, not to say desperate and even absurd. Justifying induced abortion on the basis that the fetus is not a human being or person asks us to take a lot for granted. Just because the fetus does not perform rational functions or display evidence of self-awareness does not allow us to infer that it is, therefore, not a human being or a person. The capacity to perform a particular function presupposes a nature from which that capacity flows. Snakes can't learn to ski — they lack the capacity to ski and they lack that capacity because, among other things, they are not bipeds. Their nature prevents them from acquiring that skill. Dogs can't perform mathematical calculations, read or write novels, or speculate on the meaning of life, but humans can. The difference in their respective capabilities is the difference in their respective natures.

Because function presupposes nature, I can't understand why functionalists like Mary Ann Warren and Michael Tooley are so cocksure that the human fetus is not a person and hence not a subject of rights. I have the same misgiving about the claim of Bonnie Steinbock and Peter Singer that the fetus has no moral significance until it is sentient. It is very far from clear that a being is not a legitimate member of the moral community or a person just because its potencies to think, choose, and be self-aware have yet to actualize. The snake will never ski precisely because of its snake nature; the dog will never perform mathematical calculations, or read, write or philosophize, just because of its dog's nature. So while it is fair to say that dogs, snakes, and humans *in utero* have in common the fact that none of them thinks, chooses, writes, speculates, or skis, what they don't have in common is that humans in utero *will* eventually do those things. Why? Because they are human beings, because they are persons; snakes and dogs will never do them because they are not human beings, not persons; instead, they will do what snakes and dogs do by nature of being snakes and dogs.

Given such reasonable doubt about the humanity and personhood of the fetus and given the universal moral revulsion at deliberately killing innocent human beings, I have to ask why the academic apologists for elective abortion are not afraid of being wrong and, therefore, serving as intellectual conspirators in mass murder.

And what about the policy baldly announced by Kuhse and Singer that I called attention to in Chapter 6? "We think that some infants with severe disabilities should be killed." Recall that their justification for this policy doesn't rely on the distinction between *human being* and *person*; they do not say that infants are not yet persons. Instead they create a new distinction, that between a life that is lived as opposed to a life that has not properly begun. Thus some infants can justifiably be killed because, unlike people who can understand or at least once were able to understand, an infant's life "has [not] properly begun." The authors would have their readers believe that the phrases, "before a life has properly begun" and "once a life is being lived" denote realities so different that decisions of life and death may be determined on the basis of that distinction.

The media's falsehoods and obfuscations occur chiefly in their habit of playing Ping-Pong with the words "fetus" and "unborn baby." The motive in using "fetus" is to assuage the public conscience about what induced abortion really is: the deliberate killing of an innocent and defenseless human being. But the media's pro-abortion prejudices have been exposed by David Shaw's 1990 four part series for *The Los Angeles Times*.

PREGNANCY BECOMES A DISEASE

The falsehoods and evasions of the medical profession revolve around the concept of health. Since direct abortion cures no disease, why are physicians performing abortions?

They are, after all, supposed to be healers, not killers. The late anthropologist, Margaret Mead, reportedly claimed that the "Hippocratic Oath" signaled a revolution in medicine. It has the physician swearing not to perform abortions or any other form of homicide. The revolutionary nature of the document, according to Mead, is that up until that moment in history, the physician was the medicine man: he would either heal or kill, depending on which he was paid to do. Not surprisingly, he was the most feared person in the village. Mead saw the revolutionary character of the oath in its proclamation of the physician's awareness of himself as healer, not killer.

How do physicians today reconcile this oath with their practice of abortion? The obvious, practical way is to do what they now do: many of our medical schools have abandoned the "Hippocratic Oath" in favor of oaths that do not mention abortion.

But this is a dodge, and, like all dodges, it is not sufficient to calm the moral sensibilities of those who blatantly violate the fundamental commitments of their profession. A more effective moral tranquilizer is to transform the meaning of "abortion" from killing to healing. On the very day that the U.S. Supreme Court delivered its bombshell, the *Roe v.*

Wade decision, it handed down a companion decision, *Doe v. Bolton* in which the Court defined "health" to mean "all factors – physical, emotional, psychological, familial, and the woman's age – relevant to the well-being of the patient." This is a variant of the World Health Organization's earlier definition of a "well person": "Complete physical, mental and social well-being and not merely the absence of disease or infirmity."

If you want a fuzzy definition, this is an excellent example. But it's worse than fuzzy; it's murky. Physical well-being is a straightforward concept. If I break my leg, I suffer a physical disability; the physician sets the bone and in a few weeks it mends. Mental well being is not such a straightforward concept, but that is primarily because we do not understand the psyche as well as we understand the body. This limitation lends itself to some nonsense, not to mention charlatanry and even deadly abuse. Prescribing "therapeutic" abortion to preserve a woman's mental health is an example of deadly abuse. Still, we have a reasonable, practical understanding of what mental well being and its opposite, mental illness, mean. People suffer mental breakdowns or delusions and, thanks to the psychiatrist or psychologist, they often recover to lead normal or close to normal lives. One might plausibly but erroneously confuse "social well-being" with public health. The latter is another straightforward term, signifying the branch of medicine that addresses the threat of communicable diseases by means of vaccines, quarantine, epidemiology, and the like.

The kicker in the new definition of "health" is the category of "social (or "familial") well-being." Before you ask what role the physician plays in the category, you have to find out what it means. Unlike the category of "mental health" or "mental well-being" which, despite the controversies and confusions surrounding it, retains a straightforward enough meaning at its core, the meaning of "social well-being" eludes definition the way a greased pig manages to slip through the embrace of its pursuer. It is, at best, a metaphor that makes the physician's role in diagnosing and treating it acutely ambiguous.

If there is "social well-being," there must be "social illness." But what can that mean? Would we want to say that society is losing its teeth or has become arthritic? Despite their comical sound, there are probably social conditions to which such metaphors are applicable. But who would seriously invite the physician to treat them? How would the healer of body and mind apply medical instruments of diagnosis and cure to them?

If the public fails to recognize that the concept of "health" or "well-being" as applied to body and mind is only metaphorically applied to social situations, then it might well overlook the suspicious presence of physicians in the management of "social well-being." Pro-abortion physicians would be happy if we did overlook it because the deception of "social well-being" is needed to cloak the scandal of physicians actively and willingly engaged in the practice of abortion. How can a profession committed to healing and comforting the sick justify the deliberate killing of millions of innocent human beings? The answer is simple. All you've got to do is buy into the wicked nonsense that killing "unwanted" unborn children heals "social illnesses" and thereby promotes "social well-being."

PHOTOPHOBIA AND PHOTOPHILIA

You might wonder what is so specifically vampiric about the catalog of false and misleading statements that I've just described. How, you may ask, do they get Dracula, rather than just anybody who favors abortion and infanticide, respectability?

In answer, I must repeat that I'm addressing a mythic presence in our culture. One of the conspicuous features of the vampire, as Bram Stoker depicts him, is photophobia. He shuns daylight in favor of the darkness of night. Daylight neutralizes his preternatural powers, rendering him like other human beings. In the cinematic depiction of Dracula, his photophobia becomes even more critical; it not only robs him of his powers, it kills him.

Light and darkness have, throughout history, served as symbols for truth and error as well as for good and evil. In the creation account in *Genesis,* darkness prevailed before God created the world; in the *Prologue* to John's Gospel, the entry of Christ into the world is likened to the illumination of darkness by light. And note how, in everyday language, we employ the metaphors of light and seeing to indicate understanding. We need light in order to see; thus education *enlightens* our minds so that we are enabled to see intellectually. What do we then see? The truth. As long as we remain in ignorance and error, we remain in darkness.

The photophobia that enables Count Dracula to wield his satanic powers parallels the concoctions that the pro-abortion movement needs to conceal the horror of abortion. If we can be manipulated to swallow – hook, line, and sinker – falsehoods, such as, that the human fetus is not a person, that the severely afflicted infant may be killed before it is "a life properly begun," and that abortion and infant euthanasia are medical contributions to our "social well-being," then we can be made to walk only in the night as minions of Dracula.

I take consolation in the fact that photophobia is phobic. It is the fear of the light. For all who are not vampires, which is, in any sober assessment, every human being, the light constantly beckons to us. I repeat what I said earlier in the book: Just as the eye spontaneously turns to the light, so the intellect spontaneously turns to the truth. Our human nature compels us to be photophiliacs – friends of the light and lovers of truth whether we will it or not.

Earlier I made much of the observation that, with the exception of Mary Ann Warren, my public debate opponents have doggedly avoided questions about the status of the fetus: is it a human being? Is induced abortion therefore the deliberate killing of a human being? They appeal instead to a woman's right to control her own body (despite the reality that the unborn is not part of her body) or to the personal and social "evils" of bearing an "unwanted" child (despite the glaring reduction of human life to having worth only if it is wanted or economically feasible) or neutralize the whole question, as have my opponents from the ACLU, by insisting that there's no consensus on it and thus consign it to the category of "personal belief." This is what I mean by the pro-abortionists fear of the light. They shun the truth about the unborn as Dracula shuns daylight.

All of which explains how Dracula gains respectability. Just as the vampire's prospective victim must give him entrée, must, as Twitchell observes, by some signal of acquiescence, invite him to cross the threshold of her boudoir, so do we give entrée to the vampire by tolerating lies about the nature and intrinsic dignity of unborn and infant humans.

THE VAMPIRE'S KISS

After receiving permission from his prospective victim to cross the thresh-old, the vampire's powers can be unleashed. Their effect is not always instantly destructive but can instead be gradual. In Stoker's novel, Lucy becomes a fully-fledged vampire only after weeks of nocturnal visits from Dracula. At the start, her fiancé and friends notice that something is wrong with her: she has become pale and weak, and her condition worsens by the day. Repeated transfusions of her blood, which Dracula draws from the neck wound where he has bitten her, revitalize him and weaken her.

The sexual motif here is unmistakable. He steals into her boudoir at night; he bites her on the neck; she surrenders herself to the seductive power of his "kiss." Interestingly, among Bram Stoker's contributions to the myth of the vampire is that the first time Dracula visits Lucy's bou-doir, he not only sucks her blood but opens a wound in his own chest with his fingernail and, pulling her head to the wound, forces her to drink his blood. Finally, she is completely under his domination; she is his min-ion, helpless to do otherwise than what he commands her to do. What strikes me about this sexual motif is that the wholesale elective abortions performed today are, in the vast majority of instances, done for purposes of birth control on unmarried women. They will surrender to sexual advances but not to the prospect of having babies. The movement for legal elective abortions would never have happened without the prior movement for sexual liberation.

That there comes a point of no return in this process of vampiric seduction Stoker dramatizes in the character of Mina, Lucy's assistant and friend. Dracula also bites Mina, but his program of seduction is foiled by the entrance on the scene of Dr. Van Helsing, that curious embodiment of science, religion, and superstition. Not only does he bring Mina back to full recovery, she plays the most important role of all the novel's characters in tracking Dracula down, which results in his apparent destruction by the traditionally prescribed method of transfixion. It was Mina who fig-ured out that Dracula had fled to the Continent and, thanks to the tele-pathic communication she enjoyed with the count as one of his would-be disciples, deduced his ultimate point of destination and the route he would take to get there.

In drama as in life, woman is frequently the saver of lives. That is hardly strange in light of her maternal and nurturing nature. She sponta-neously protects human life, especially when that life is helpless. In cases of consensual sex, women are in control, contrary to feminists like Sally Markowitz who insist they are driven to abortion because the Federal government refuses to underwrite women's contraception even though men have targeted women for the satisfaction of their lusts. It is the woman who decides whether there will be sex or not and if there will be an abortion. Giraudoux gives powerful dramatic expression to the maternal protective urge in the second act of his play, *Ondine:*

> *Bertha:*The bird was in my hand, Majesty. He [Bertha's fiancé] pressed my hand so hard that the bird was killed.

> *Ondine*: He did not. A woman's hand, no matter how soft, becomes a shell of iron when it protects a living thing. If the bird were in my hand, Your Majesty, Hercules himself could press with all his strength and never hurt it.

I'd like to parallel this account to the progress of the anti-life movement. Back in the late 1950s, when arguments for liberalized abortion laws began to emerge on the public scene, they almost always appealed to the hard cases: the mother will die if she carries the pregnancy to term; the baby will be born deformed; if the woman is forced to carry the child of her rapist, she will suffer serious psychological harm, and so forth. Once the public accepted these appeals to "humanitarianism," it had, in fact, affirmed, at least implicitly, that a human being may be used as a mere means to an end rather than an end in himself; for they'd given the green light to the deliberate killing of the innocent. Let me repeat (for the nth time) that I've never been persuaded by pro-abortionists who insist that they really believe the unborn is not a human person.

Once you affirm that a human being may be used as a mere means to an end, you will find it increasingly difficult to show why that principle can't be applied to cases other than abortion. To affirm that a human being is a mere means to an end is to affirm, whether you like it or not, that it is not intrinsically evil to deliberately kill the innocent and, therefore, that the decision to do so depends on circumstances rather than the dignity of the human person.

Should we be surprised, then, that we have traveled from legalizing abortion for the hard cases to legalizing elective abortion? Should we be surprised that our intellectuals, especially the professors of philosophy, have proceeded from the moral justification of abortion to the moral justification of infanticide and eldercide? Bob Edwards, the embryologist who, with the late Patrick Steptoe, produced Louise Brown by in vitro fertilization in 1978, recently predicted: "Soon it will be a sin of parents to have a child that carries the heavy burden of genetic disease." We have given the vampire social respectability by persuading ourselves that unborn and infant humans are expendable for humanitarian concerns. At first, these concerns were for the welfare of the woman or unwanted child yet to be born; then they were for the suffering of a hopelessly afflicted child allowed to live and for the suffering the parents would experience should they be forced to raise the child, like the "Johns Hopkins baby." That was the case where the parents refused permission for surgical correction of their newborn child's inability to swallow food or drink, preferring to let him die of dehydration fifteen days later, because he was born with Down's syndrome. Finally, our concerns were for the welfare of a society that must bear the burden of supporting severely afflicted human beings.

I'll put my own suspicions aside, and simply say that it would be illuminating to find out how many of these concerns are really for the well-being of the child and how many are simply for the parents and society. What I mean is, how many concerns are not really to free the child from his misery but to free us from the child's misery?

I'll be the first to admit that any attempt to locate the vampire myth in our culture solely on the basis of the above examples looks like a stretch. But abortion is a necessary prelude to compelling examples of the myth's presence that serve as a backdrop for the destruction of the helpless in hopes of our own regeneration. Consider again, the transplantation of fetal tissue to other human beings, not to mention the efforts of some physicians and legislators to change state laws so that anencephalic infants can be declared brain dead at birth, thereby allowing their organs to be harvested immediately for transplantation and the "Pittsburgh Protocol" that drastically shortens patients' resuscitation time before declaring death, making their organs more accessible for transplantation. In force at the University of Pittsburgh's Medical Center since 1992, the Protocol permits the removal of the patient's organs in as few as two minutes after heart death. Thus is the demand increasing for human organs; thus was

Dracula's unquenchable demand for human blood.

Interesting to me is that in Stoker's story, Lucy begins her bloodsucking apprenticeship by killing children and from there proceeds to work her way to journeyman status by preying on adults, the first being her attempt on her fiancé. This parallels the close connection between elective abortion and fetal tissue transplants. Fetal tissue is ideally suited for transplants because its nascent, totipotent structure reduces the possibility of rejection by the recipient's body. Although prospects that the transplantation of fetal nervous tissue to adults suffering from Parkinson's disease and fetal pancreatic tissue to diabetes patients will produce a cure or at least a significant improvement in the recipient's condition have recently been dampened by rather indifferent results, the recent breakthrough in methods for harvesting embryo stem cells seems to have blinded many researchers to the growing evidence for the successful use of stem cells harvested from umbilical cords and the bone marrow of adults. As I stated at the beginning of this chapter, the message persists that the reliable source for these cells can be none other than the fetuses from elective abortions or embryos discarded from the petri dish.

Tell me if you do not think it vampiric to seek to maintain our lives by harvesting the tissue of those we directly kill. Is it not an exact parallel with Dracula's killing his victims in order to make their blood his own and thereby become younger and stronger? We've already had a case in Phoenix where a woman purposely got pregnant so that she could abort her unborn child and then transplant tissue from its nervous system to the brain of her father who suffers from Parkinson's disease. With almost a million-and-a-half legal abortions performed yearly in the United States alone, the emergence of a fetal transplant industry, not to mention the sale of fetal parts, was inevitable. And it promises to be a very lucrative venture. For example, the Geron Corporation of California, which has perfected the use of embryo stem cells to create cloned human tissues for adults, in 1999, paid Rosslin Institute, which cloned Dolly, $25.9 million in stock to form Geron BioMed. Surely, if you can morally justify the deliberate killing of the unborn, you can, with complete consistency, justify the transplantation of the victim's tissue and make a handsome profit while you're at it. A spinal cord sells for $325, a reproductive organ for $550, and a brain for $999. Dracula epitomizes the whole process: he not only revitalizes himself by killing others, he gains immortality. This is the essence of our own abortion culture: we stand on the threshold of harvesting the tissue and organs of unborn, infant, and adult humans, hoping to regain our health and youth – and even achieve immortality.

Maybe the seeming golden promise of unending youth will eclipse the public perception of the wickedness of abortion. Consider the following passage from a piece by Lori Brannigan Kelly whose father suffers from Parkinson's disease.

> The promotion of fetal implants does not, in and of itself, legitimate abortion. But exploiting the fetus – albeit toward a positive end – certainly helps relax our consciences to the point where the heinousness of abortion becomes a non-issue. As Neuhaus points out, medical ethicists stand ready, with the courts as willing accomplices, "to produce ever more sophisticated rationalizations for turning the unthinkable into the routinely doable." The speed with which such rationalizations develop is always inversely proportional to the present strength of society's moral fiber. Thus, we must fear that fetal harvesting and research will proceed with unchallenged momentum. If propelled by the success of Parkinson's transplants and motivated by results, the results-motivated medical community will further shift the focus of the abortion debate off the wrongfulness of the act, highlighting instead the tremendous benefits of fetal implants. Such a shift will legitimate a logic wherein abortion is less and less considered a grave and reprehensible evil, and more and more a "regrettable event" that can nevertheless deliver a positive outcome.

Abortion and infanticide are at the same time realities and symbols. Lucy begins her vampiric career by attacking children, but consider that children symbolize vitality and optimism. Her apprenticeship as a vampire mirrors the rationale for the culture of death. Stoker has Dracula leading Jonathan Harker to believe that his interest in moving to London is primarily to expand his real estate holdings. The truth is that Dracula is aging and losing his strength because he has sucked Transylvania dry; its inhabitants have become old and effete. He needs new, young blood and hopes to find it in England, which he sees as the New World. We, too, suck the blood of others for our own enrichment. How? By spilling the blood of the unborn for our own convenience, our careers, our economic or psychological stability, our whatever.

And like Dracula's minion, Lucy, our killing moves us through the stages of life as we move from apprentices to journeymen in our killing. We started by killing the newest of our race, the unborn, then moved on to infanticide and now want to kill our burdensome aged to restore economic vitality.

THE ILLUSION OF VAMPIRIC IMMORTALITY

Our fascination with vampires is large. Almost five thousand movies have been made about them; Ann Rice's vampire novels are always bestsellers; and the vampire is found in the literature of both the east and west from antiquity down to today. Can the abortion culture learn an important lesson about its direction and future prospects from the myth of the vampire? I think so.

No doubt this continuous fascination stems largely from the vampire's singularly terrifying character. The colorful and idiosyncratic English priest, Montague Summers, opens his classic study of vampires, *The Vampire, His Kith and Kin*, with the following observation:

> Throughout the whole vast shadow world of ghosts and demons, there is no figure so terrible, no figure so dreaded and abhorred, yet dight with such fearful fascination, as the vampire, who is himself neither ghost nor demon, but yet who partakes the dark natures and possesses the mysterious and terrible qualities of both.

But despite his terrifying nature, I find the vampire a pathetic creature. It's not just his nocturnal confinement that makes him pathetic. Of course, it is a significant limitation to be able to roam about at full steam only after sundown and, in daylight, to be reduced to the status of a mere mortal, at best, and, at worst, to be destroyed by the light.

I find Dracula pathetic chiefly because his preoccupation enslaves him. He has gained immortality. You might suppose that if you had all that time ahead of you, you could exploit limitless possibilities of exploration and self-enrichment. But does Dracula visit foreign lands and exotic places to slake his curiosity and broaden his outlook? Does he live a life of leisure and study? Does he labor to make the world a place of beauty and justice? There is no need to multiply examples. The answer to these questions is "No." He is compelled to spend the waking hours of his immortal life desperately searching out victims who will supply him with blood.

This transfusion of blood from his victims to himself revitalizes him. But for what? For one thing only. Blood sucking gives him the strength to suck more blood. Bram Stoker does allude several times in the novel to Count Dracula's assiduous study habits. But it becomes clear that he pursues knowledge not for its own sake but so that, by better understanding the world, he can more efficiently track and seduce his prey. The immortality that Dracula has bought himself is an endless life in a squirrel cage: he seeks blood in order to live and he lives in order to seek blood. Blood is not gasoline for his journey through eternity or to happiness; blood is his very destination, the be-and-end-all of his life. Dracula cannot die, but he cannot live, either, in any desirable sense of that word. The pathetic fact is that the enslaver is the enslaved.

This reflection inspires the final parallel that I wish to draw between the vampire and our exploitation of unborn and infant human beings. I'll introduce it by drawing upon another assessment of McNally and Florescu in their book, *In Search of Dracula*. They characterize the vampire's existence as both frightening and tragic, for it is a life devoid of hope, peace, or fulfillment. He needs to drink the blood of others if he is to continue his existence; yet he knows he cannot choose to die. Thus his desire to go on living is as compulsive as his search for blood. His lack of hope, peace, and fulfillment comes down to this: he wants to live, yet he wants to die; he does not truly live, but he is not truly dead. All the vampire myths, the authors contend, inevitably reveal that our fear of death cannot eclipse our fear of things greater than death.

This assessment can be applied to our culture: unlike the vampire, we can die, but our fear of death prevents us from accepting it. By "fear of death," I'm not talking about the natural fear of it but the exaggerated fear that draws its strength from a materialistic outlook. If all life and striving are reducible to biological existence and material goods, then death is the complete and final cancellation of all meaning and value.

Faced with such a grim prospect, killing the innocent and defenseless and cannibalizing their body parts are attractive and plausible gambits. After all, they promise to extend the only thing that we, as materialists, can count on – this worldly existence. In this regard, I find it significant that traditionally the vampire – even the aristocratic Count Dracula – is characterized as having a putrid smell about him, the sign of arrested decay.

Life is important, but ambiguously so. Truly, it is important in itself just to be alive, as opposed to not existing at all. Life is also the presupposition for humanizing ourselves and reaching our ultimate destiny. What about the ambiguity? That appears in the struggle of a being, created for better and higher things than merely material goods and a long, healthy life, to invest all his or her energy and hope to gain those very evanescent things. That agenda can only generate frustration and end in death.

Physical death is one thing. When I said that I found the putrid smell attributed to the vampire's arrested decay to be significant, I was thinking about its symbolism. In analogous fashion, you can detect arrested decay in the spiritual death of a being composed of body and spirit who subverts its higher, spiritual self for its lower, bodily self: "Do not fear those that kill the body alone but those that can kill both body and spirit." It is the paradox of the human person that when he tries to save his life he loses it and when he loses his life, he gains it. Just as the vampire is not really living but *nonliving* and *undead*, pathetically suspended between life and death, so the society that would seek to avoid death by feeding off the innocent finds itself trapped in the frustration of the city of the undead. Its inhabitants have reduced themselves to *revenants*, creatures who are miserable in life and fearful of death. Imagine an endless life consisting of living simply to go on living. Wouldn't we all end up shouting, "This, this, more of this again, only this!"

The frustration of Dracula is the frustration of the anti-life society. The source of the frustration lurks in the vampire's photophobia. Living in the absence of light, both Dracula and the anti-life society live in the absence of truth – the darkness of falsehood and lies. Aristotle's unsurpassed definition of "truth" and "falsity" contain the seeds of vampiric frustration: "Truth is to say of that which is, that it is, and of that which is not, that it is not; falsity is to say of that which is that it is not and of that which is not that it is." The life that Dracula has sold his soul to purchase is the illusion of life. Illusion because it has mistaken that which is not for that which is.

I alluded to the vampire's inability to conquer his victim all at once, to how that conquest requires stages of submission to him. Even now, despite the millions of abortions performed in the United States, it is not too late to rally from Dracula's initial bites. Mina recovered and went on to be the principal agent of his destruction.

Still, as long as history continues, we'll never conquer evil decisively and finally. At the end of Stoker's *Dracula*, Jonathan Harker shears Dracula's throat while Morris plunges his bowie knife into the vampire's heart; the monster emits a blood-curdling scream and immediately decomposes into a heap of dust. Was he thus destroyed, once and for all? I'm not so sure. It is, after all, a characteristic power of the vampire to transform himself into smoke. Was the billowing dust that seemed to mark Dracula's demise, the end of him? Or do you think he's since slipped back among us, this time to oversee physician-assisted suicide and human cloning? Maybe the billowing dust was his getaway smoke.

APPENDIX A

The following account and critique of my debate with Professor Mary Ann Warren appeared in the November 30, 1979 edition of the University of San Francisco's school paper, *The San Francisco Foghorn.* The author, Chris Smith, was then a freshman. I present the piece without comment, except to call attention to two points: First, the obvious difference in my view of what I said and emphasized and Mr. Smith's view. He clearly found Warren's argument more interesting than mine; second, his misconstrual of my use of Aristotle's definition of "man" as *rational animal:*

> It is not at all uncommon for a debate on abortion to become an emo-tional, irrational shouting match. But last Tuesday, Nov. 20th, USF hosted a true debate; one involving not rhetoricians, but people well grounded in logic. The speakers were Dr. Mary Ann Warren and Dr. Raymond Dennehy. Taking the pro-choice argument, Dr. Warren gave a very clear presentation of her views. On the other hand, Dr. Dennehy took a pro-life side and appeared to have gotten the better of the discussion (according to the audience, which was probably biased).
>
> The debate was well attended, by an obviously blood-thirsty pro-life crowd. Originally to be held in McLaren 250, the room had to be enlarged by opening the partition that separates it from McLaren 251.
>
> The format of the discussion was as follows. Each speaker made a 5-minute statement of position, followed by rebuttals from both sides. Then, a number of questions were put to the speakers. At first, they were answering ques-tions for which they had already prepared answers. Later, these questions came from the audience, and the two speakers had to ad lib.
>
> The forum opened with Dr. Dennehy's statement of position. Dr. Dennehy began by identifying one of the most important aspects of a democratic society: The protection of the innocent in their right to life. He then went on to show that the fetus is a separate human being, and is "not part of the mother's body in any defensible sense." Dr. Dennehy concluded his argu-ment by naming abortion as something which "sounds the death-knell of

democratic society."

Dr. Warren's turn came next. She astutely narrowed the argument down to one point, and based most of her arguments on it. She asserted (quite correctly) that the central issue is whether or not the fetus has rights. If so, she admitted the fetus must be accorded the full protection of the law. On the other hand, if the fetus does *not* have the right to life, then it is (*sic*) possible development into a child is at the mercy of the mother. One technique Dr. Warren exploited was the comparison of the fetus to lower forms of life. She contended that until the fetus exhibits significant differences from these forms of life, it is legally and morally equivalent to dogs, fish, and monkeys. And since the fetus doesn't become "significantly different" from lower forms of life until "shortly after birth," the fetus can be destroyed at any time up to, and shortly after birth, and the mother's decision to do this need not be justified in any way at all.

Each speaker had the opportunity to contest the statement of the other. Dr. Warren had the first shot. While she agreed with Dr. Dennehy that fetuses are human beings, Dr. Warren stated that status as a human being does not confer on an individual fetus "the full-fledged right to life." She defined a person as a human being with certain minimal mental capacities, without which it does not sufficiently differ from other forms of life. In addition, she said "...If you take the rights of people seriously, you have to take the rights of women seriously, and that to deny a woman the right to choose whether or not she wants to bear a child, is to violate her most fundamental rights. It is a very, very serious moral wrong."

Dr. Dennehy then had his chance to dispute Dr. Warren's statement. He started by disputing Dr. Warren's claim that there are two kinds of human beings; persons and non-persons. He found it "fantastic" that a fetus – a "non-person," according to Dr. Warren – suddenly blossoms into a human being which manifests signs of "personhood." Dr. Dennehy continued, "...if it occurs from within (the change from non-person to person), it is merely an unfolding of what is already there ...it is no essential change, but merely a fulfillment of what the being is already. If it occurs from outside, then I would ask for an efficient cause, an explanation of what changes that lowly fetus into a person." This appeared to have been a crucial part of the argument, perhaps meriting further debate. The conclusion of Dr. Dennehy's rebuttal referred to Dr. Warren's assertion that the women's rights are uppermost. Dr. Dennehy countered her argument with a historical, legal precedent: That the rights of one person end as soon as they abridge the rights of others.

The statements and rebuttals having been delivered, the questions began. The first question: "Is the fetus a human being, and what do you mean by this?" Dr. Warren responded first. Her answer was somewhat vague. She began by naming two "relevant" senses of the word "human being." In the first sense, the "genetic sense," the fetus is a human being. However, in the "moral sense" (the "genetic sense" being "irrelevant" to the discussion) the fetus is *not* human. She also limited human rights as belonging to "... only beings which want to live..." She mentioned that, "...if this seems less than fully evident, I think it's largely because we tend to confuse ... the distinction between the senses of the word or fail to make the distinction at all."

Dr. Dennehy's answer to the question was slightly more direct. He began by defining "human being," and limiting the possible meanings of the term to one: Aristotle's "rational animal." Whereas Dr. Warren made the primary criteria for "personhood" mental, Dr. Dennehy mentioned that a human being is not mere intellect: because that would put him in the realm of God and the angels. Consequently, intellect cannot be a criterion for judgment, according to Dr. Dennehy. This seems to be a concession to Dr. Warren's claim that the fetus is not rational. But Aristotle's definition of a human being seems to call for rationality, which doesn't exist in the fetus (according to Dr. Warren). What Dr. Dennehy apparently wound up with is the fact that the fetus is not a human being in any sense of the word, whereas Dr. Warren agreed that a fetus is "genetically" a human being.

The second question, answered first by Dr. Dennehy: "Does the mother have the right to abort a fetus?" His answer: ... no. Nobody has the right to take innocent human life, under *any* circumstances." He continued, basically stating that, "The right to life must be the primary right." Dr. Warren responded to this question by disapproving of the words used in the question. She felt that a "mother" was a woman who had brought a pregnancy to term, and that the words "pregnant woman" would be more accurate. She then went on to state that a woman does have the right to abort a fetus without restrictions (in the first trimester) and that poverty constitutes a restriction. It was in answer to this question that she reemphasized the mother's total release from having to justify this move.

The next question, fielded by Dr. Warren: "Are economic and other factors, such as overcrowding, delinquency, and child abuse adequate reasons to permit abortions?" Her answer was a qualified "Yes," saying that abortion is justified only if we have determined whether or not the fetus is a person."

Dr. Dennehy, faced with the same question, said, "No. It seems to me that economics and urban design...exist for the benefit of persons." He stated that to kill persons for these reasons is an "inversion of values; you've turned the world upside down."

The fourth question: "Are physical and mental limitations adequate reasons to permit abortions?" Dr. Dennehy answered that such limitations do not change one's status as a human being.

Dr. Warren's view: "...if the *mother* has some physical or mental limitation, this is a fully adequate reason for her to choose abortion." Similarly, if a *child* is likely to have such a limitation, "this is also a sound reason for choosing abortion... the woman has at least some *moral obligation* to consider the possibility of abortion.

Dr. Warren received the next question. "Does the justification for abortion lend itself to the justification of euthanasia and infanticide?" Dr. Warren evaded this question rather neatly. She first mentioned that there are many so-called "justifications" for abortion, not all of which justify infanticide or euthanasia. She did, however, eventually get around to *her* justification for abortion: The non-personhood of the fetus. She then addressed the topic of euthanasia, and whether the prospective victims are persons. She stated the example of a comatose man who had no hope of regaining consciousness. She then tried to prove that such a man was in fact a person, saying that "...all his neurological machinery is intact...so he is just an unconscious person, and has rights as such."

Dr. Dennehy, replying to the same question, cited the case of Dr. Waddell, a Los Angeles doctor charged with manually strangling a baby he attempted to abort. His defense consisted of asserting that, "...if a woman has the right to murder the child...it shouldn't matter whether it is done on this side of the womb, or that side of the womb." This seems to be a justification for infanticide.

There were many questions from the audience, most trying to logically contradict some particular statement made by Dr. Warren. They can be summed up in a few questions I asked of myself.

Dr. Warren notes that a human fetus is intellectually equivalent to other life forms, and therefore deserves to be treated as such. In a manner of speaking, Dr. Warren was saying that the fetus should not have human rights, because it is intellectually indistinguishable from other life forms. Why is the intellectual aspect of the fetus the only "relevant" one? Should not the fetus be equivalent to these other life forms in *every* respect for her argument to hold?

One question was asked several times by the audience: "When does this sudden change take place?" (From non-person into person.). Though Dr. Warren asserted that no such change *does* take place – that it happens slowly – there can be no middle ground. That is, the fetus is either a person or not a person, and the change from one to the other *must* be instantaneous. This has a tremendous impact on Dr. Warren's nebulous definition of when a non-person becomes a person: "Shortly after birth."

Consider Dr. Warren's criteria for personhood: "Certain basic mental capacities." Perhaps a fetus lacks these "capabilities" because he has no need for them. In the protected environment of the womb, of what use are "the will to live" and "self-consciousness?" If one believes that everything in nature has a purpose, an intellectually developed fetus certainly poses a problem: What is the purpose of an intellect in such an environment, when there's nothing to exercise it on?

Also, Dr. Warren made a distinction between "genetic" humanity and "moral" humanity, stating that the moral sense of the word is the *only* relevant one. This is as doubtful as it is arbitrary: Why is the "genetic" sense of the word irrelevant?

Finally, Dr. Warren, in stating that her justification for abortion does not justify euthanasia, mentioned that a fetus is different from a comatose man. She said that the unconscious man is a person, and that the fetus is not, the basis for decision being one's neurologic state. The man is a person because "... his faculties aren't operating, but they are intact. By intact, I mean they *could* function." But the faculties of a fetus not only "could" bloom into operation – like those of the unconscious man – they probably will!

While debates like this seem to serve little purpose, they actually do influence people's position. Several people, previously bewildered by the emotional arguments traditionally used in this dispute, now have clear concepts of the issue they are dealing with. It is debates like this one that make the truth much easier to discover.

APPENDIX B

The following letters are samples of the 46 letters sent me by students enrolled in the IDS 130 class at the University of California, Berkeley in the Spring Semester of 2000. The students are required to write a letter to one of the speakers who visited the course. Each week different speakers visited to speak on different topics. That explains why, out of 700 students, I received only 46. I was surprised to find that a slight majority favored my position. 19 accepted it; 17 rejected it, and 12 had mixed reactions. I excluded from the sample letters that were vindictive or merely rhetorical. No attempt has been made to edit the letters.

UNFAVORABLE

May 3, 2000

Dear Mr. Dennehy,
Thank you for coming and speaking to us on the topic of abortion. I enjoyed your presentation and found your argument both compelling and eloquent. However, I cannot agree with a premise of your argument, and therefore cannot agree with your argument.

From what I gathered from you presentation, your argument is based on the premise that the fetus is alive upon conception. This premise is, to put it euphemistically, contested by many people.

Although I found your philosophical argument sound and logically correct, I find the foundation of your argument, this premise that the fetus is alive upon conception, somewhat suspect. If at some time in the near future some scientists discover evidence that validates this premise without uncertainty, then clearly you should jump on this vindication and make your argument heard loud and clear. However, until then, I am not convinced that the fetus is alive at the point of conception, and neither should you. Moreover, until then, I believe we must address abortion in a realistic manner in the sense that, like it or not, it continues to occur, despite potential philosophical arguments against it such as yours. Your argument in particular depends on scientific validation, which is yet to be discovered.

Thank you,

[Signed]

Dr. Dennehy,
As you know we are required to write a letter to one of the speakers. I chose to write to you, because of all the speakers your argument was the most polished, logical and structurally sound. I guess all the years of practice helps. Before I continue, let me restate what I understood to be your point: Abortion is the deliberate killing of an innocent human being. Furthermore, democracy is impossible with such immoral actions. If this is false then you can toss this letter in the garbage and save your time. Your whole argument is based on the assumption, or opinion, that killing an innocent human being is necessarily immoral. Yet not once did you address why this is so. You spent a lot of time demonstrating that a fetus is life and a human being, but is that not already common knowledge? Of course the unborn child is innocent; it has not had the opportunity to do anything. Abortion is definitely deliberate since the mother goes to the clinic with the expressed purpose removing the baby. As far as the whole democracy issue goes, I guess then that in the history of human kind there never has been a democracy or a society that fits such ideals. Human life has never been valued above all else, to list as examples: war, capital punishment, duels, human sacrifice. Ah, but the victims were either not innocent or the killing of them was not deliberate (except for in case of human sacrifice.) Regardless, that is beside the point, the point is the

assumption of immorality. Nobody can claim that killing is immoral. Every human on this earth, by the very
fact that they are alive, has killed. We have to kill just to
stay alive, how else can we eat? Every food product is
derived from the taking of life. Every human construction destroys life. Biologically speaking, in the early stages
of fetal development there is not a whole lot of difference between the fetus of an ape and a human. Why
then do we put such an importance on Human life? There
are plenty of humans out there, in all reality there are too
many humans. To say it is immoral to kill an innocent
unborn human is not different than to say that it is immoral to give children up for adoption or to raise them
in an environment in which they will be malnourished
or abused, which are normally the options other than
abortion. I could just as easily assert it is immoral to
contribute to the growth of a population that will eventually destroy the very world that supports it. As you can
read I am pro-abortion. This stance is not because I do
not believe that abortion is killing an unborn child, but
rather because I have no moral objections to it. Basically
I am suggesting that in order to make your presentation
more effective in convincing people like myself to stop
abortion, you need to address the substrate upon which
your argument is constructed.

Sincerely,

[Signed]

Dear Mr. Dennehy,
I would first of all like to state that I thoroughly enjoyed
hearing you express you stance on the abortion issue.
Although I am pro-choice, I think you brought up some
important points that I had not thought of before. However, I found that although your reasons are very educated and logical, you failed to sufficiently address the

most important reason for abortion.– practicality. That is, the reasons why a woman might need to have an abortion outweigh the philosophical arguments against it. When you consider the negative impact that an unwanted child could have on the mother (and, sometimes, the father), such as losing her job, social life, and ability to grow as a person, and contentment with life in general, the philosophical "moral" reasons supporting your argument against abortion become trivial. In your lecture you asked if the basis of right to life depends on being wanted, and for reasons of practicality, I think the answer is yes. You said that there are approximately 1,500,000 legal abortions each year. I see this statistic as meaning that the births of 1,500,000 children who are unwanted and probably destined to lead unhappy lives are avoided each year, and I think it is awful that there are so many women who need abortions but do not seek them because of reasons pertaining to religion or the law.

Unfortunately, Ms… could not provide as persuasive an argument as you. She apparently lacks the good argumentative skills that a Ph.D. in Philosophy would have. If it had been a debate, then you clearly would have won. I would like to conclude this letter by restating that although I do not agree with your opinion about abortion, I think that your argument is compelling and should be considered by people who are pro-choice and pro-life alike. Thank you.

Sincerely

An anonymous Student from the Spring 2000 IDS Class.

FAVORABLE

May 5th, 2000

Dear Dr. Dennehy,

I would like to thank you for taking time out and speaking about abortion to the IDS 130 "Issues in Health and Medicine" lecture on February 7th. I enjoyed your lecture and your arguments immensely. You brought great enthusiasm and confidence. You are firm in you beliefs and had great supportive examples.

However, your line of reasoning, the logic behind it all, is complex yet brought into a simple context in which we are able to understand and follow through. I believe that this is your biggest strength in your argument. You almost left us no choice but to agree with you. I suppose that this is where your doctor of philosophy is expressed. Your rhetoric is comparable to that of Plato's rhetoric in "The Allegory of the Cave." Your questions and reasoning lead us along a path, and when we have come full circle, we end up with the same perspective as yours. For me the worst part of it all is that I am pro-choice, but I found myself at the end of your lecture shaking my head and saying "Geez, he's right." I should have expected that you have the ability to turn heads since you are, after all in the front line of the battle between pro-choice and pro-life. However, though I am still pro-choice, I would have to say that you have, by far, made a more convincing argument for pro-life than anyone else I have heard or read. I find almost no flaws in your arguments and reasoning. Although pro-choice activists will have their own line of defense, it is difficult if not impossible to take offense and attack your arguments because there are no glaring weaknesses.

I feel that you can make your arguments stronger by offering your perspective about one more issue on abortion. If abortion is to be made illegal and all women are forced to carry out their pregnancy, how can society handle this? You argue that the mistake of the woman cannot be erased by the murder of an unborn child. However, should a child be born, both the child and the mother would surely lead a much harsher life. The social

welfare of the entire society would plummet with many
women unable to support themselves and their children.
This is the common defense of pro-choice activists, and
if you are able to directly combat this line of defense,
your arguments would surely be more convincing.

Once again, I would like to thank you for your time.
Your professionalism is much appreciated. I hope to hear
you speak again sometime in the near future.

Sincerely,

[Signed]

Dear Mr. Dennehy,
First off, I would like to thank you for coming to speak
to our class and give us your views on why abortion
should be illegal. The lecture you gave about abortion
was very thought provoking and had me thinking for
days after about what you had said. Being at a school like
Berkeley, one does not ordinarily come across a speaker
who has the views that you espouse. I think what made
your presentation so impressive was the organization and
the facts that you had to back up what you said. The
woman who argued against you also had facts, but hers
were just numbers with not much substance (at least that
is how I felt). However, everything that you used as
evidence was explained in a thorough and well-orga-
nized manner. Even someone who was completely
against your overall premises, they could not argue the
facts that you put before the class, whether the person
was pro-life or pro-choice. Thinking about all that you
had said made me really start to wonder why I had soft-
ened my stance on abortion and kind of stay on the fence
about what I thought was right. No one should have to
go through the pain and agony of having to decide
whether or not to end their pregnancy. It is a decision
that should not even enter their heads because I think

that it should not be a practice that is lawful. There were people who argued that people would do it anyway if it was unlawful and you brought up the point that most would obey the law since an overwhelming majority of people are for the most part law-abiding citizens. The only question that I have for you is that while I agree with your basic underlying, that aborting a fetus is the killing of another human being, I think that it would be helpful if you talked about alternatives for people, especially young people, whether abortion is legal or not. Overall you presentation really struck a cord with me and continues to do so.

[Signed]

May 1, 2000

Dear Dr. Dennehy,

Thank you for a very interesting and thought provoking lecture. Indeed, all your arguments were compelling and critical. Despite what some argued, the arguments, I believe, were not only philosophical, but also scientific and from real life. I also appreciated the honest instead of the use of twisted language. For instance the other speaker in the same lecture, kept using the expression Anti-Choice to describe people who are not Pro-Choice. Does that make her Anti-Life since she is not Pro-life? That kind of twisted language, although it has a major effect when addressing 10 year olds, it is not as effective when addressing the students of one the major universities in the world.

Although pictorial illustrations are often used against pro-life activists, with the argument that they use human emotions to achieve their goals, I think some illustrations (not too many) would have been a good addition to the presentation. Maybe something about partial-birth, or a segment of any of the videos that show the horrors of abortion.

An argument that was made during the discussion sections by some students and TA's was that your argument is good and one can't oppose it or effectively argue against it, but to them still obviously (although it's hard to argue it) the mother should have some choice! I would suggest more emphasis on the practicality of the arguments, in other words, that this is not only a philosophical discussion (with all respect to philosophy)!

Finally, I would like to suggest offering us ways on campus for those interested to help promote pro-life ideals. Many student organizations should be willing to sponsor something like this. Also, I would suggest publicizing it as a debate on campus, long enough before the actual lecture, to allow more students and student organizations on both ends of the spectrum to participate. Usually at Berkeley the lecture hall space is not crucial, since they have the ability to have the lecture broadcast live in another lecture hall for those who are willing to only watch it without interactive participation.

Once again, I would like to thank you for one of the best lectures in the course, and wish you success in your mission.

Sincerely,

[Signed]

MIXED RESPONSES

Thank you for presenting a very argumentative speech on one of the most controversial topics facing our society today. Your speech was greatly appreciated by me as well as, I am sure, by many others. The most engaging aspect of your talk was the fact that you argued the so-called pro-life point of view without bringing in the issue of

religion and its teaching. Personally, I have never witnessed such a stance and I am sure this holds true for many
others. I believe that many members of society find themselves opposing religion rather than the pro-life position
in making the decision to "be pro-choice." Partially, I
have been one of these people. I say partially because I
remember the fear of pregnancy during my teenage years
being as strong as that of a kind of plague, sometimes stronger than the fear of sexually transmitted diseases. I remember how thankful I was to have the option of having
an abortion even though I tried very hard to escape the
plague of an unwanted pregnancy. On a more impersonal
level however, I was not going to allow myself to agree
with the religious fanatics who show films of slaughtered
unborn babies at county fairs in the Midwest. So in this
way I was opposing religious fanaticism and not the pro-
life view. Therefore, I thank you again for flawlessly defending the pro-life point of view argumentatively.

I say that your justification was flawless because as I sat and
carefully listened to your talk, I subconsciously sought flaws.
I am a person of logic. Opinions do not convince me,
logic does. Therefore, as I have been a firm believer in
abortion, your reasoning disconcerted me. I guess you
may say that you "achieved your goal." You have convinced me that abortion is a form of murder. However, I
still believe in it. I now believe in murder. The reason that
I still believe in abortion is the fact that I could not justify
forcing a raped woman to carry the pregnancy to term.
So your talk has left me convinced yet frustrated. I would
have liked you to have taken the issue further and consider it on a realistic, rather than a theoretic level. I would
like to know how you would deal with the issue if it were
up to you to make the rules by which we live as a society.
I would like to know how you would change the law and
justify the inequality between men and women that would
result from making abortion illegal. I realize that you are
a philosopher and theory is what is of interest to you.
However, I hope that you agree that when your theory
meets reality, the world will become a better place.

Sincerely,

[Signed]

April 19, 2000

Dear Dr. Dennehy,

Thank you very much for speaking to my class. I found your talk to be quite interesting and stimulating; your arguments are very clear and rarely heard. The vast majority of those vocally opposed to abortion do so on religious grounds. Also, they often have ready solutions, like constitutional amendments or specific restrictions on the procedure. I found that the argument based solely from a philosophical perspective to be refreshing. This may be because as I take more biology courses, the more I feel inclined to agree with your argument that a human being is a human being regardless of the stage of development. Additionally, because your arguments are based on scientific fact, they make more sense and are more convincing than those based on rhetoric, as much of the abortion debate on both sides has become. However, most anti-abortionists seemingly never use such an argument, perhaps thinking of any scientific perspectives as irrelevant and unnecessary.

However, I don't fully agree with your viewpoint, probably because I find myself unable to view the situation as being fully philosophical in nature. I am male, and as such, I feel that I can't fully appreciate some aspects of being female, and of course I assume the reverse is true. As is, I feel that although I am, on some levels, opposed to abortion, I don't feel that I could impose my beliefs on anyone else. Which, again, deviates from the speculative nature of this argument, but I have difficulty separating the philosophical from the practical.

As much as I enjoyed the lecture, I felt that some things

didn't go so well....[The CARAL speaker raised some good points, but they unfortunately had little to do with your speech. I imagine this is primarily due to those organizing the lectures, but it was nonetheless a shame not see too much debate of ideas. Also, I felt that some questioners were openly hostile to both of you, which I thought was generally a waste of time. But regardless, thank you for coming and talking to us; I enjoyed your speech and it is still making me think.

Sincerely

[Signed]

May 2, 2000

Dear Dr. Dennehy,
Thank you for coming and talking to our class. I was very interested in the manner that you approached the subject of abortion. Before the lecture I had not put much thought to the subject of abortion. Your lecture and my class discussion made me aware of the deep feelings that people have on the subject. I honestly have mixed feelings about where I stand on the subject of abortion. My fiancée and I have discussed the subject before and have agreed that we do not agree with abortion in our family. Where I am torn is in pressing my opinion on others. I find it very difficult to impose restrictions on the bodies of others. Your argument for the life of a baby made this decision more difficult. I am unclear where the rights of one individual end and the rights of another begin. I have difficulty imposing my beliefs on others because I fear regulating human beings. I know that in many other countries the rights we take for granted are not available.

Dr. Dennehy, I personally feel that many of the problems that are associated with abortion are due to people not being well informed of their choices. Many people that are against abortion are also against contraceptives. We should work in making contraceptives available to young people, hopefully preventing the subject of abortion from ever coming up. I don't clearly remember what your stand is regarding contraceptives, but I feel that it is an error in judgment by many to want to stop abortions, but also to stop the use of contraceptives. For those unfortunate people that do have an unwanted pregnancy, I feel that they are often not given sufficient information regarding the choices they have other than abortion. People should be as informed as possible to be able to make a wise decision regarding their life and the life of another.

As you can see, I do not have a strong stand on abortion, but thank you because your lecture actually made me think more about the subject. After class I spoke to other students and family as to where they stood on the subject. What I found is that people are very firm about what they believe, but are often so involved with their feelings that they miss the logic on the other side. Hopefully your lecture proved to be as thought provoking for others as it was for me.

Sincerely,

[Signed]

REFERENCES

CHAPTER ONE:

H.Tristram Engelhardt,"Medicine and the Concept of Person," *Contemporary Issues in Bioethics*, ed. By Tom L. Beauchamp & Leroy Walters (Belmont, CA:Wadsworth Publishing Company, 1982)

Germain Grisez, *Abortion: the Myths, the Realities, and the Arguments* (New York, N.Y.: Corpus Books, 1970)

John T. Noonan, Jr., "An Almost Absolute Value in History," *The Morality of Abortion: Legal and Historical Perspectives*, ed. by John T. Noonan, Jr. (Cambridge, Mass.: Harvard University Press, 1970)

Michael Tooley, "Abortion and Infanticide," *Philosophy and Public Affairs* 2/1 (1972)

Mary Ann Warren, "On The Moral and Legal Status of Abortion," *The Monist*,Vol. 57, #1 (January, 1973); also found in a number of anthologies on bioethics and abortion.

CHAPTER TWO:

Raymond Dennehy, "The Social Encyclicals and the 'Population Bomb'," *Social Justice Review*, October, 1972

Paul Ehrlich, *The Population Bomb*, rev. ed. (Rivercity, Mass.: Rivercity, 1971)

Garrett Hardin, *Exploring New Ethics for Survival: The Voyage of the Spaceship Beagle* (New York: Penguin Books, 1976)

_____,"The Tragedy of the Commons," *Science*, December 13, 1968

"A New Ethic for Medicine and Society" (editorial), The Journal of *California Medicine* (now titled *The Journal of Western Medicine*), 113 (1970)

Re For the California Supreme Court decision on fetus murder: *People v. Davis, 872 P.2d 591 (Cal. 1994);* also Katherine B. Folger, "When Does Life Begin…or End? The California Supreme Court Redefines Fetal Murder in People *v.* Davis" *University of San Francisco Law Review* Volume 29 #1 Fall, 1994, 237-277

Judith Jarvis Thomson, "A Defense of Abortion," *Philosophy and Public Affairs*, Vol. 1 #1 (Fall, 1971); also found in a number of anthologies on bioethics and abortion.

Michael Tooley, *Abortion and Infanticide* (Oxford: Clarendon Press, 1983)

Dr. J.C. & Mrs. Willke, *Handbook on Abortion* (Cincinnati: Hayes Publishing Company, Inc., 1971)

CHAPTER THREE

Sally Markowitz, "A Feminist Defense of Abortion," *Social Theory and Practice* vol. 16, 1 (Spring, 1990); also in *The Abortion Controversy*, ed. By Louis P. Pojman and Francis J. Beckwith (Belmont, CA: Wadsworth Publishing Company, 1998)

Bernard Nathanson, M.D., "Confessions of an Ex-Abortionist," http://www.aboutabortions.com/Confess.htn; see also his book, *Aborting America* (Garden City, N.Y.: Doubleday, 1979)

CHAPTER FOUR

Helga Khuse & Peter Singer, *Should the Baby Live?* (Oxford: Oxford University Press, 1985), *Preface*

CHAPTER FIVE

Re experiments on severed fetal heads: "Post-Abortion Fetal Study Stirs Storm" *Medical World News*, January 8, 1973

CHAPTER SIX

Re quotes from Lincoln: quoted in Hadley Arkes, *First Things: An Inquiry Into The First Principles of Morals and Justice* (Princeton, N.J.: Princeton University Press, 1986), pp.24-25, 43-44.

Encyclopedia Britannica, Vol. 6, p. 184

Bruce M. Carlson, *Patten's Foundations of Embryology*, 5th ed. (New York: McGraw-Hill Book Company, 1988), p.3

R. O'Rahilly, "One Hundred Years of Human Embryology," *Issues and Reviews in Teratology*, 1988, 4: 81-128

Robert Joyce, "Personhood and the Conception Event," *The New Scholasticism*, (now titled *The American Catholic Philosophical Association Journal*) Vol. 52 #1 (Winter, 1978)

Lee M. Silver, *Remaking Eden* (New York, NY: Avon Books Inc., 1997), pp. 25-26 & 48

Williams Obstetrics, 17th ed. Jack A. Pritchard, Paul C. MacDonald,

Norman F. Gant (Norwalk, Conn.: Appleton-Century-Crofts, 1985), p. 139

R. Yanagimachi, "Mammalian Fertilization," *The Physiology of Reproduction*, E. Krobil, J. Neill, *et al.* ed. [New York: Raven Press, 1988], p. 115

CHAPTER SEVEN

Carl L. Becker, *The Declaration of Independence* (New York: Vintage Books, 1942)

Re Peter Singer and infanticide: Raymond Dennehy, "Grading the Professor" *National Catholic Register*, April 25-May 1, 1999

Joseph J. Ellis, *The Founding Brothers* (New York: Alfred A. Knopf, 2000)

Germain Grisez, "When Do People Begin," *Abortion: A New Generation of Catholic Responses*, ed. Stephen J. Heaney (Braintree, Mass.: The Pope John Center, 1992), p. 5

Fredric Wertham, M.D., *A Sign For Cain: An Exploration of Human Violence* (New York: The Macmillan Company, 1966) Chapter One

CHAPTER EIGHT

Paul Barber, *Vampires, Burial, and Death* (New Haven & London: Yale University Press, 1988)

Re Dr. Bob Edward's prediction that soon it will be regarded as a "sin" for parents to give birth to child with genetic defects: *The Observer*, May 9, 1999

Re Gentec's purchase of the Rosslin Institute: *The London Sunday Times*, July 7, 1999

Re Fetal parts for sale: ABC press release 20/20 March 6, 2000: also check various websites under that topic.

Jean Giraudoux, *Ondine*, Act II in *Four Plays*. Adapted by Maurice Valeny (New York: Hill and Wang, 1958) (2 vols.), Vol. 1

Lori B. Brannigan Kelly, "The Ethics of Fetal Transplants," *The Human Life Review*, Vol. 15 #1 (Winter, 1989)

Raymond T. McNally & Radu Florescu, *In Search of Dracula* (Greenwich, Connecticut: New York Graphic Society, 1972), p. 190

Re Margaret Mead's claim that the Hippocratic Oath signaled a revolution in medicine: Maurice Levine, M.D., *Psychiatry and Ethics* (New York: Braziller, 1972), pp. 324-25 & 377.

David Shaw, *The Los Angeles Times*, July 1-4, 1990

Wesley Smith, *The Culture of Death* (San Francisco: Encounter Books, 2000), 160-165

Bram Stoker, *Dracula* (Garden City, N.Y.: Garden City Books, 1959?)

Montague Summers, *The Vampire, His Kith and Kin* (New Hyde Park, N.Y.: University Books, 1960), p.1

James B. Twitchell, *The Living Dead: A Study of the Vampire in Romantic Literature* (Durham, North Caroline: Duke University Press, 1981), p.10

INDEX